RECORD BREAKERS
Machines and Inventions

For a free color catalog describing Gareth Stevens Publishing's list of
high-quality books and multimedia programs, call 1-800-542-2595 (USA) or
1-800-461-9120 (Canada). Gareth Stevens Publishing's Fax: (414) 225-0377.
See our catalog, too, on the World Wide Web: http://gsinc.com

Library of Congress Cataloging-in-Publication Data

Lafferty, Peter.
      Machines and inventions / written by Peter Lafferty.
          p. cm. -- (Record breakers)
      Includes index.
      Summary: Describes a variety of record-breaking machines and
inventions, including the fastest train, the first mechanical clock,
and the largest airships ever built.
      ISBN 0-8368-1950-0 (lib. bdg.)
      1. Inventions--History--Juvenile literature.   2. Machinery--
History--Juvenile literature. [1. Inventions.   2. Machinery.]
I. Title. II. Series.
T15.L16 1997   97-6170
609--dc21   9695

First published in North America in 1997 by
Gareth Stevens Publishing
1555 North RiverCenter Drive, Suite 201
Milwaukee, Wisconsin 53212 USA

First published in 1994 by Watts Books, 96 Leonard Street, London, England, EC2A
4RH. Original © 1994 Orpheus Books Ltd. Text consultant: Dr. Trevor Williams.
Illustrations by Sebastian Quigley (Linden Artists), Alan Weston (Kathy Jakeman
Illustration), Roger Stewart, and Martin Woodward. Photo acknowledgements:
8tr Science Photo Library; 8cl Harry Ransom Humanities Research Center, The
University of Texas at Austin; 8c Société Française de Photographie; 9l Gilman Paper
Company Collection, New York; 9c Science Museum; 9r Royal Photographic Society;
31 Hulton-Deutsch Collection. Additional end matter © 1997 Gareth Stevens, Inc.

Printed in the United States of America

1 2 3 4 5 6 7 8 9 01 00 99 98 97

RECORD BREAKERS

Machines and Inventions

by Peter Lafferty

Gareth Stevens Publishing
MILWAUKEE

CONTENTS

Words that appear in the glossary are in **boldface** type the first time they occur in the text.

INTRODUCTION

IN 1987, A TRAIN CARRIED PASSENGERS at 249 miles
(400 kilometers) per hour — a world speed record. The train
never touched the track as it hurtled along. It was supported in the
air by a magnetic field. Meanwhile, the United States space probe
Pioneer 10, launched in 1972 on a journey to take photographs of
Jupiter, has now left our Solar System and is more than 4,970 million
miles (8,000 million km) from Earth. It is the most remote, Earth-
made object in existence. The Hubble Space Telescope is sending
back to Earth detailed pictures of galaxies that are thousands of
billions of miles in the distance. This telescope is so powerful, it
could detect light from a flashlight 248,560 miles (400,000 km) away.

As technology advances, more and more astonishing records like
these will be broken. The first machines seemed just as impressive to
people hundreds of years ago. The first passenger-carrying vehicle,
a steam-powered wagon built in 1769, reached the grand speed of
1.9 miles (3 km) per hour. But it still managed to take part in the
world's first traffic accident when it crashed into a wall.

This book is a log of the extraordinary, record-breaking achieve-
ments made in the field of scientific technology.

THE FIRST MECHANICAL CLOCK
AND OTHER GREAT CHINESE INVENTIONS

IF YOU BUY THIS BOOK with paper money, put up an umbrella, strike a match, fly a kite, or push a wheelbarrow, you have China to thank. These items are so familiar we scarcely wonder where they came from. But they were invented in China.

The iron plow, steel manufacturing, printing, the rocket, and many more inventions were developed by the Chinese many centuries before these extraordinary things appeared in the West. The mechanical clock (*see opposite*), magnetic compass, suspension bridge, playing cards, parachute, paddle-wheel boat, even the decimal system — all first appeared in China long ago.

Some of these inventions found their way to Europe through reports from travelers, while others were later "invented" by Europeans unaware

that they already existed. Without inventions that originated in China, Europe in the Middle Ages might have been a very different place. Seed drills, iron plows, collar harnesses, and the technique of growing crops in rows — ideas imported to Europe from China — helped farmers. The magnetic compass, the ship's rudder, and other nautical improvements guided European explorers across the world's oceans in the fifteenth century. Gunpowder greatly strengthened armies. Printing presses spread knowledge around the world. All these inventions come from China.

From late medieval times onward, far fewer inventions have come out of China. Since then, most technological advances have been made in Europe, North America, and Japan.

The first machine to record earthquakes, called a **seismograph** (*right*), was invented in A.D. 132. When the machine is shaken, a rod inside it swings

and opens one of eight dragons' jaws. A ball drops into the toad's mouth below, recording the direction of the earthquake.

Invented in the first century B.C., the Chinese wheelbarrow needs much less effort to move than modern designs. The weight is balanced evenly on both sides of the wheel.

GREAT CHINESE FIRSTS

Magnetic compass **4th century** B.C. *Known in Europe, 11th century*

Paper **2nd century** B.C. *Known in Europe, 12th century*

Rudder **1st century** A.D. *Adopted by Europeans, about 1180*

Suspension bridge **1st century** A.D. *Suspension bridge built in United States, 1801*

Fishing reel **3rd century** A.D. *Known in Europe, 17th century*

Umbrella **4th century** A.D. *Known in Europe, 18th century*

Matches **6th century** A.D. *Made in Europe, 19th century*

Printing **8th century** A.D. *First European presses, 14th century*

Playing cards **9th century** A.D. *Known in Europe, 13th century*

Paper money **9th century** A.D. *Made in Sweden, 1661*

Gunpowder **9th century** A.D. *Used in Europe, 13th century*

Rocket **12th century** A.D. *Made in Europe, 14th century*

SU SONG'S COSMIC ENGINE

The world's first mechanical clock was built by a Buddhist monk named Yi Xing in A.D. 725. It was a vertical waterwheel with cups, instead of paddles, fixed to its blades. The wheel turned when one of the cups was filled with water. The weight then became too heavy for a pin holding it steady, and the wheel moved forward one notch. It was then held by a pin until the next cup was filled, and so on. Rods and gears attached to the wheel moved the "hands" that told the time.

Yi Xing's clock went out of use soon after it was built. Years later, Su Song's clock of 1092 (*left*), which had a similar mechanism, ran for nearly fifty years. Detailed descriptions were written about the 40-foot (12-meter)-tall clock. The wheel drove two globes for observing the positions of the stars. It also drove a five-story pagoda in which different figures appeared at the window to point out the hours of the day.

Su Song's great clock (*above*), showing the mechanism inside.

When a cup was full in Yi Xing's clock (*above*), it pressed on a lever that pulled open the lock at the top of the wheel. The wheel turned, and a new cup was filled.

THE FIRST PHOTOGRAPH
NIÉPCE'S HISTORIC IMAGE

THE EARLIEST PHOTOGRAPH that survives today was taken in 1827 by a Frenchman named Joseph Nicéphore Niépce. Simple cameras had been invented centuries earlier. In these cameras, rays of light reflected from an object passed through a pinhole in a dark box to make an upside-down image on a screen inside. But the problem was how to make the image permanent. Niépce solved the puzzle by fitting his camera with a metal plate coated with a thin layer of a substance called bitumen-and-oil. After eight hours, a ghostly image formed on the plate. The quality of photographic images was improved by another Frenchman, Louis Daguerre, and an Englishman, William Fox Talbot.

X rays were discovered accidentally by German scientist Wilhelm Röntgen in 1895. These invisible rays can pass through many materials, such as flesh, but not through metal or bone. Röntgen made the first X-ray photograph *(right)* of his wife's hand in 1896. Her ring is clearly visible.

The earliest surviving photograph was a view taken in 1827 by Joseph Nicéphore Niépce from the window of his home near Beaune, France.

Louis-Jacques-Mandé Daguerre's photo of an artist's studio was the world's first fully successful photograph (1837). It was called a **daguerreotype**, a photograph produced on a copper plate.

When American inventor George Eastman introduced the easy-to-use Kodak camera *(right)* in 1888, photography became popular. Eastman also produced the first roll films.

THE FIRST MOVIES

In 1891, American inventor Thomas Alva Edison (*see page 10*) built a machine called the Kinetoscope. It was the first successful moving-picture machine. Only one person at a time could view a movie through an eyepiece as a sequence of photographs on a strip of film wound past. Just four years later, two brothers, Auguste and Louis Lumière, presented the first public cinema showing in a cafe in Paris. The films showed scenes of everyday life in the city.

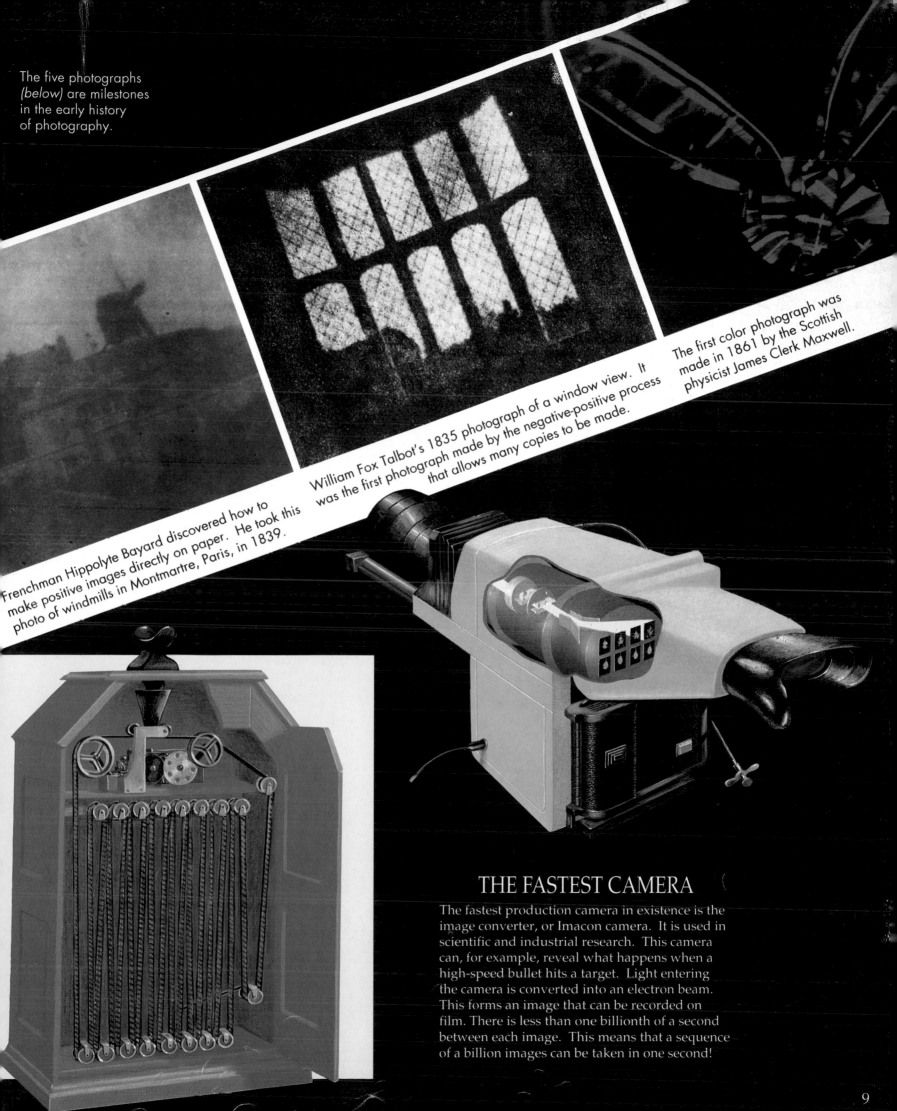

The five photographs *(below)* are milestones in the early history of photography.

William Fox Talbot's 1835 photograph of a window view. It was the first photograph made by the negative-positive process that allows many copies to be made.

The first color photograph was made in 1861 by the Scottish physicist James Clerk Maxwell.

Frenchman Hippolyte Bayard discovered how to make positive images directly on paper. He took this photo of windmills in Montmartre, Paris, in 1839.

THE FASTEST CAMERA

The fastest production camera in existence is the image converter, or Imacon camera. It is used in scientific and industrial research. This camera can, for example, reveal what happens when a high-speed bullet hits a target. Light entering the camera is converted into an electron beam. This forms an image that can be recorded on film. There is less than one billionth of a second between each image. This means that a sequence of a billion images can be taken in one second!

TALKING MACHINES

In March, 1876, American inventor Alexander Graham Bell made the world's first telephone call. Over a telephone in the next room, Bell's assistant, Thomas Watson, heard the words, "Mr. Watson, come here, I want you." In Bell's telephone, there was a steel strip that vibrated when someone spoke close to it. These vibrations were sent along a wire with an electric current to make another strip vibrate, reproducing the original sounds. The sounds were not very clear. Users of the first telephones had to shout to make themselves heard.

The telephone was improved by another American inventor, Thomas Alva Edison, so that it could be used over long distances. Edison also adapted some of the telephone's parts to produce the first recording machine that he called the phonograph. The first recorded sound was heard in 1877, when Edison listened to his own voice saying "Halloo, Halloo!"

Edison's phonograph was like a telephone, only with the vibrating parts connected to a steel needle. As Edison spoke into a horn, the needle "wrote" the pattern of vibrations on a piece of foil wrapped around a drum that was turned at the same time. When the needle was brought back to the beginning of its written message and the drum turned again, the pattern in the foil made vibrations in the same way. The telephone parts vibrated, and the sound came back out the drum.

In this imaginary scene, five great inventors are gathered around a table with their famous inventions.

ALEXANDER GRAHAM BELL
First telephone (1876)

THOMAS EDISON
First recording machine (1877)

First electric light bulb (1879) (also invented by Joseph Swan)

GUGLIELMO MARCONI
First radio transmission across Atlantic (1901)

MESSAGES WITHOUT WIRES

Radio waves carry radio sounds and television pictures. They move through the air at the speed of light. Heinrich Hertz, a German physicist, sent the first radio signals over a short distance in 1887. Italian inventor Guglielmo Marconi showed that radio messages could be sent across the world. In 1901, Marconi sent the first transatlantic radio signal — the three dots of *S* in Morse code — from Cornwall, England, to Newfoundland in Canada, a distance of 2,187 miles (3,520 km).

SAMUEL MORSE

FIRST WITH THE NEWS
GREAT ELECTRICAL INVENTIONS

THE TELEPHONE, television, and radio are a big part of our daily lives. Yet not much longer than 150 years ago, they did not even exist. The very first machine for sending messages was not electrical at all, but a tower with great mechanical arms on top of it. The arms could be moved into different positions, each standing for a different word or number. Series of towers were built within sight of one another between two places. Their operators relayed messages from one tower to the next. These "semaphore telegraphs" first appeared in France in the 1790s.

First electric telegraph that recorded messages on paper (1838)

JOHN LOGIE BAIRD
First television pictures (1926)

The Scottish inventor John Logie Baird was the first to give a demonstration about television in 1926. His camera used a spinning disk pierced with holes and an electronic "eye." The eye recorded the brightness of different parts of an image — the head of a ventriloquist's dummy — and transmitted what it "saw" to a screen.

11

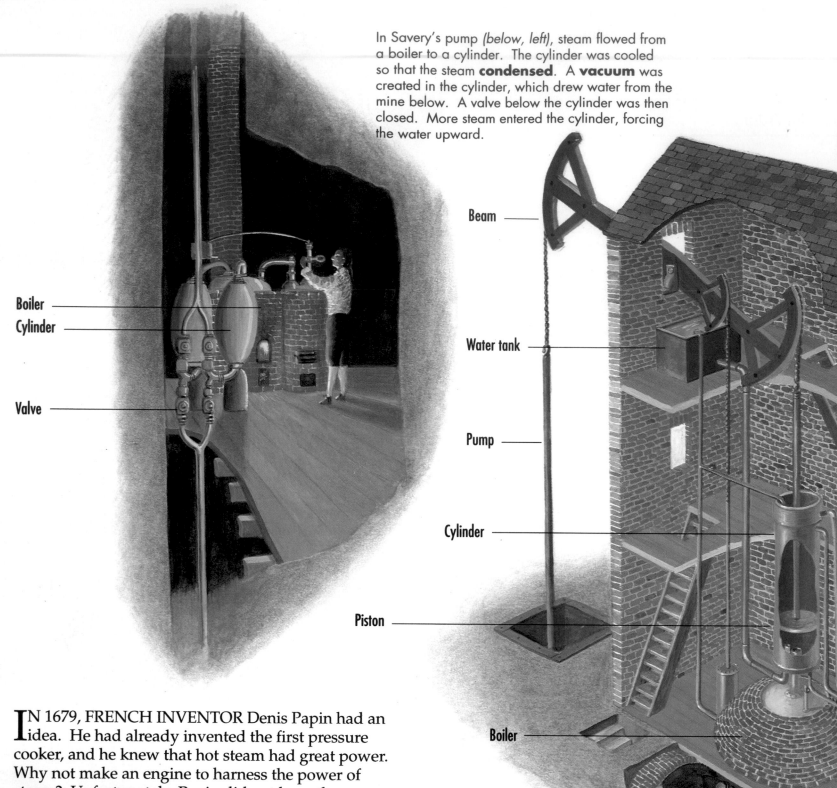

In Savery's pump *(below, left)*, steam flowed from a boiler to a cylinder. The cylinder was cooled so that the steam **condensed**. A **vacuum** was created in the cylinder, which drew water from the mine below. A valve below the cylinder was then closed. More steam entered the cylinder, forcing the water upward.

Boiler

Cylinder

Valve

Beam

Water tank

Pump

Cylinder

Piston

Boiler

IN 1679, FRENCH INVENTOR Denis Papin had an idea. He had already invented the first pressure cooker, and he knew that hot steam had great power. Why not make an engine to harness the power of steam? Unfortunately, Papin did not have the money to develop his idea. He died in poverty in 1714.

The first steam engine was designed in 1698 by Thomas Savery, an English engineer. It was called "the miner's friend" because it was built to pump water out of mines. Its only known successful use, however, was in lifting water in large houses in London, England.

The first working steam engine was built in 1712 by the English engineer Thomas Newcomen. A large beam rocked back and forth sixteen times a minute as the machine pumped water. In 1776, James Watt, a Scottish instrument maker, improved the Newcomen engine. His engines did not waste as much heat and made better use of the power of steam.

Newcomen's engine *(above)* used **atmospheric pressure** not to draw up water but to drive down a piston. Steam was admitted to a cylinder at a pressure high enough to push up the piston inside it. The steam was then condensed by a spray of water, a vacuum was created, and atmospheric pressure drove the piston downward. The movement of the piston rocked the beam back and forth and operated the pump.

THE FIRST STEAM ENGINES
DRIVING FORCE OF THE INDUSTRIAL REVOLUTION

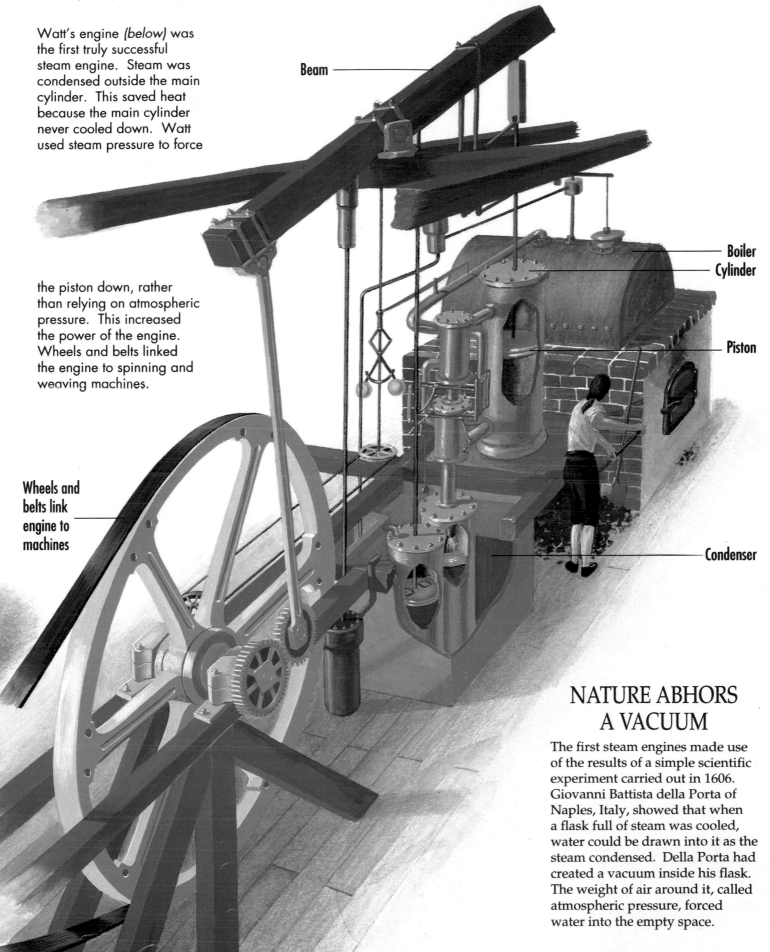

Watt's engine *(below)* was the first truly successful steam engine. Steam was condensed outside the main cylinder. This saved heat because the main cylinder never cooled down. Watt used steam pressure to force the piston down, rather than relying on atmospheric pressure. This increased the power of the engine. Wheels and belts linked the engine to spinning and weaving machines.

Beam

Boiler

Cylinder

Piston

Condenser

Wheels and belts link engine to machines

NATURE ABHORS A VACUUM

The first steam engines made use of the results of a simple scientific experiment carried out in 1606. Giovanni Battista della Porta of Naples, Italy, showed that when a flask full of steam was cooled, water could be drawn into it as the steam condensed. Della Porta had created a vacuum inside his flask. The weight of air around it, called atmospheric pressure, forced water into the empty space.

THE LARGEST LOCOMOTIVE
UNION PACIFIC'S "BIG BOY"

THE LARGEST, HEAVIEST and most powerful railroad locomotive that ever pulled a train was called the "Big Boy." Between 1941 and 1945, twenty-five of these giants were built by the American Locomotive Company of Schenectady, New York, for the Union Pacific Railroad. They were 131 feet (40 m) long (about 1.5 times the length of a basketball court) and weighed more than 661 tons (600 metric tons). Each locomotive was able to haul a load six times its own weight up a steep grade in the mountains of the western United States.

Big Boys had two sets of eight driving wheels. The front set was specially designed to swivel to enable the giant locomotive to go around bends on the twisting mountain railway. No worker could shovel coal fast enough to keep the furnace stoked, so a mechanical stoker was used. This machine could deliver 24 tons (22 metric tons) of coal an hour to the firebox. The Big Boys used a lot of water, too. At top speed, they guzzled 55 tons (50 metric tons) of water an hour.

Illustrations are approximately to scale.

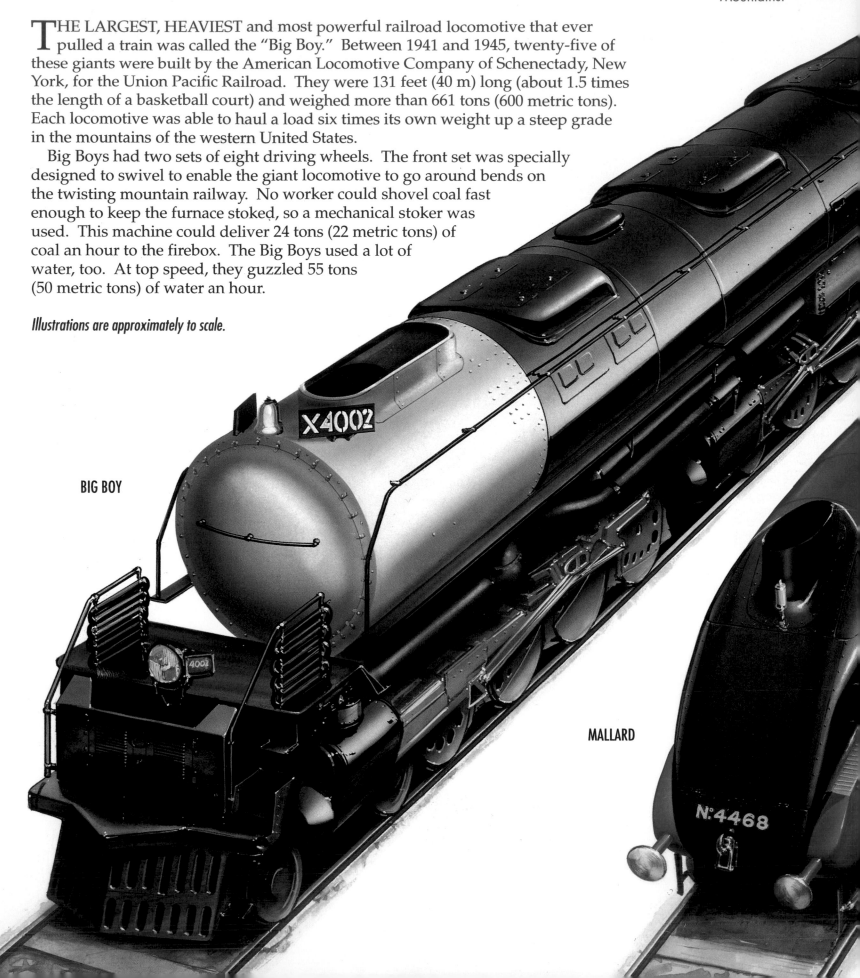

BIG BOY

MALLARD

THE FASTEST STEAM LOCOMOTIVE

A new world speed record for a steam locomotive was set on July 3, 1938. The Mallard *(left)*, a new engine fitted with a streamlined casing, was chosen for the honor. Pulling a seven-coach train between Grantham and Peterborough, England, the Mallard was timed at a speed of 125 miles (201.16 km) per hour over a distance of about 1,312 feet (400 m). It was damaged during the run but was repaired and placed in the Railway Museum in York, England. Its record has stood to this day.

TREVITHICK'S LOCOMOTIVE

THE FIRST TRAINS

The first steam locomotive to run on rails was built by English engineer Richard Trevithick. His four-wheel locomotive *(left)* made a demonstration run on February 22, 1804, reaching 12.5 miles (20 km) per hour when empty and 5 miles (8 km) per hour when loaded. Unfortunately, the weight of the train broke the rails! By 1812, stronger tracks had been built between Middleton Colliery and Leeds, England. They carried the first successful steam locomotives. In 1829, while the new Liverpool and Manchester Railway was being built in northern England, a contest was held to find the best locomotive to travel it. The contest was won easily by a locomotive called the Rocket *(left)*, entered by George and Robert Stephenson. It reached the then breathtaking speed of 29 miles (46.7 km) per hour, a world record. For the first time, people would be able to travel on land faster by train than horse.

This illustration *(below)* shows the inside of a steam locomotive. Water is heated by fire tubes in the boiler. The steam is forced into a cylinder, where it pushes a piston linked to the driving wheels. When the piston reaches the end of the cylinder, steam is let into the other side, pushing the piston back again.

ROCKET

Boiler · Steam · Piston · Firebox · Driving wheels · Cylinder

THE FASTEST TRAIN
FRANCE'S ROCKET ON RAILS

THE FRENCH HIGH-SPEED TRAIN, the Train à Grande Vitesse or TGV, holds the world speed record for a train traveling on rails. During a test run without passengers between Paris and Tours in 1990, the TGV reached a speed of 320 miles (515 km) per hour, or more than 1.5 times the speed of a Formula 1 racing car (see page 44). Even in regular service, the TGV easily outpaces any other train. The 264-mile (425-km) journey from Paris to Lyon takes only two hours.

The TGV is powered by electric current from an overhead cable. It has two locomotives, one at each end of the train. Its eight passenger cars are all carefully streamlined, so the train uses up no more power than an ordinary train.

Back in the age of steam trains, workers in the driver's cab faced a panel of dials and levers. They felt searing heat from the firebox, and their ears were nearly deafened by the pounding noise. The TGV driver's cab is more like a modern office, the noise of the speeding locomotive barely rising above the level of whirring computers. Computers effectively drive the train. The driver checks the train's progress on a computer screen and types instructions on a keyboard. A radio links on-board computers with a signaling center and other trains on the track. Computers also operate the brakes, air-conditioning, and other equipment.

The high-speed TGV can travel up slopes four times as steep as most other trains. Therefore, tracks built for it can be much straighter, saving on the cost of construction over hilly country.

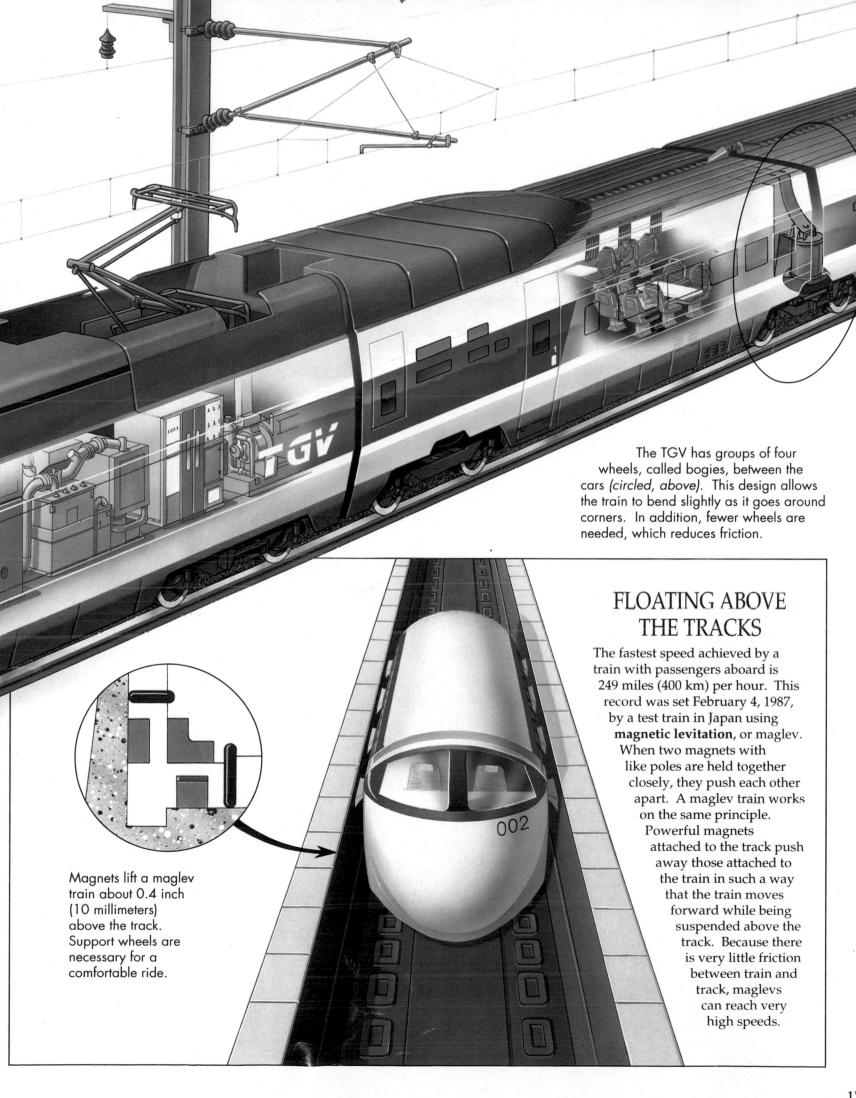

The TGV has groups of four wheels, called bogies, between the cars *(circled, above)*. This design allows the train to bend slightly as it goes around corners. In addition, fewer wheels are needed, which reduces friction.

FLOATING ABOVE THE TRACKS

The fastest speed achieved by a train with passengers aboard is 249 miles (400 km) per hour. This record was set February 4, 1987, by a test train in Japan using **magnetic levitation**, or maglev. When two magnets with like poles are held together closely, they push each other apart. A maglev train works on the same principle. Powerful magnets attached to the track push away those attached to the train in such a way that the train moves forward while being suspended above the track. Because there is very little friction between train and track, maglevs can reach very high speeds.

Magnets lift a maglev train about 0.4 inch (10 millimeters) above the track. Support wheels are necessary for a comfortable ride.

002

RACING YACH

BLUE WHALE

The Typhoon class submarines *(above)* from the former Soviet Union are the largest submarines ever built. They can stay under water for years at a time. They were designed to carry missiles that could strike targets 5,600 miles (9,000 km) away.

The largest ocean liner of all time was the *Queen Elizabeth (above).* Launched during World War II, she began service as a troop ship. After the war, the ship was used as a cruiser.

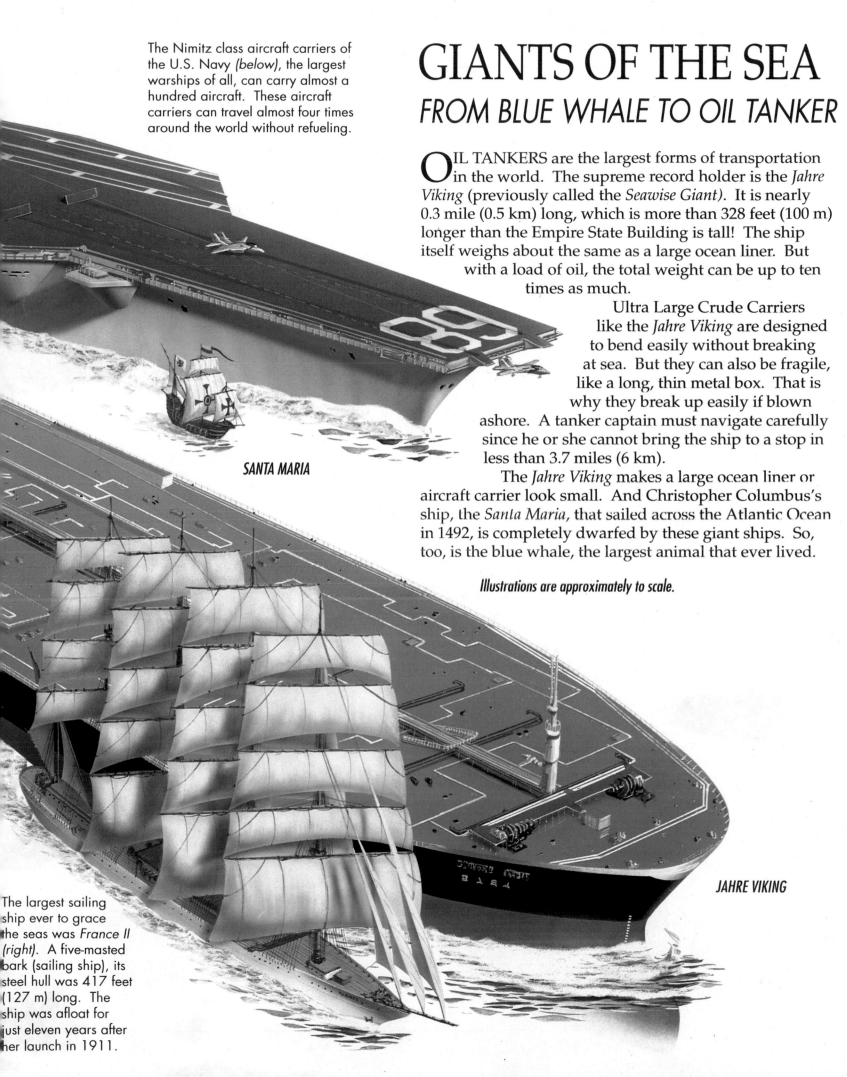

The Nimitz class aircraft carriers of the U.S. Navy *(below)*, the largest warships of all, can carry almost a hundred aircraft. These aircraft carriers can travel almost four times around the world without refueling.

GIANTS OF THE SEA
FROM BLUE WHALE TO OIL TANKER

OIL TANKERS are the largest forms of transportation in the world. The supreme record holder is the *Jahre Viking* (previously called the *Seawise Giant*). It is nearly 0.3 mile (0.5 km) long, which is more than 328 feet (100 m) longer than the Empire State Building is tall! The ship itself weighs about the same as a large ocean liner. But with a load of oil, the total weight can be up to ten times as much.

Ultra Large Crude Carriers like the *Jahre Viking* are designed to bend easily without breaking at sea. But they can also be fragile, like a long, thin metal box. That is why they break up easily if blown ashore. A tanker captain must navigate carefully since he or she cannot bring the ship to a stop in less than 3.7 miles (6 km).

The *Jahre Viking* makes a large ocean liner or aircraft carrier look small. And Christopher Columbus's ship, the *Santa Maria*, that sailed across the Atlantic Ocean in 1492, is completely dwarfed by these giant ships. So, too, is the blue whale, the largest animal that ever lived.

Illustrations are approximately to scale.

SANTA MARIA

The largest sailing ship ever to grace the seas was *France II (right)*. A five-masted bark (sailing ship), its steel hull was 417 feet (127 m) long. The ship was afloat for just eleven years after her launch in 1911.

JAHRE VIKING

19

HUMAN-POWERED VEHICLES
FROM RUNNING MACHINE TO FLYING MACHINE

PEOPLE FLED IN TERROR and horses bolted when Baron von Drais first rode his "running machine" in 1817. The German inventor sat astride his *draisienne*, which consisted of two wheels, one behind the other, connected by a wooden frame. He moved the machine forward by pushing on the ground with his feet. On good roads, the machine was faster than a horse. It was the fastest land vehicle of its time.

The *draisienne* was the first of a long line of human-powered vehicles, eventually leading to the first human-powered aircraft. In 1839, a Scottish blacksmith, Kirkpatrick Macmillan, built the first real bicycle — one that could be driven without the rider's feet touching the ground. It had pedals that turned the back wheel. Macmillan was fined five shillings

when he knocked over a child during a ride through the city streets.

The first truly successful pedal-powered bicycle was made in Paris in 1861 by a coach repairer, Pierre Michaux, and his son, Ernest. They fitted two pedals to the front wheel of a *draisienne*. This new machine, known as a "boneshaker," became very popular. English inventor James Starley designed a bicycle in 1870 that became known as the Penny Farthing. It had an enormous front wheel 5 feet (1.5 m) across and a much smaller rear wheel. Starley later built the Rover safety bicycle. With its diamond-shaped frame, equal-sized wheels, and geared chain drive, this 1885 machine was the forerunner of modern bicycles.

Macmillan's bicycle *(left)* had pedals connected with rods to the back wheel. Ernest Michaux's first "boneshaker" *(right)* had wooden or iron wheels that, as the name suggests, made riding uncomfortable. John Boyd Dunlop of Belfast, Northern

Ireland, introduced air-filled tires in 1888. The Starley Rover *(right)* had a chain connecting the pedals to the back wheel.

PEDALING THROUGH THE AIR

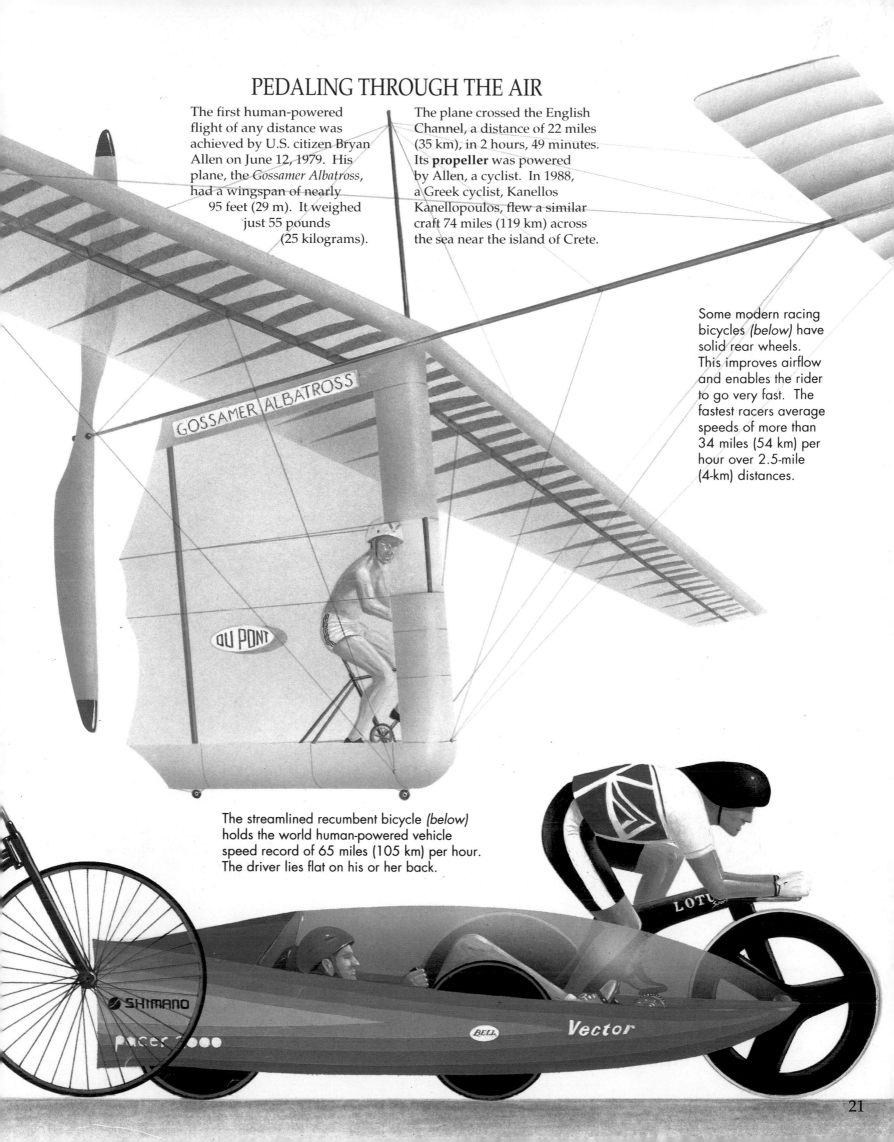

The first human-powered flight of any distance was achieved by U.S. citizen Bryan Allen on June 12, 1979. His plane, the *Gossamer Albatross*, had a wingspan of nearly 95 feet (29 m). It weighed just 55 pounds (25 kilograms).

The plane crossed the English Channel, a distance of 22 miles (35 km), in 2 hours, 49 minutes. Its **propeller** was powered by Allen, a cyclist. In 1988, a Greek cyclist, Kanellos Kanellopoulos, flew a similar craft 74 miles (119 km) across the sea near the island of Crete.

Some modern racing bicycles *(below)* have solid rear wheels. This improves airflow and enables the rider to go very fast. The fastest racers average speeds of more than 34 miles (54 km) per hour over 2.5-mile (4-km) distances.

GOSSAMER ALBATROSS

DU PONT

The streamlined recumbent bicycle *(below)* holds the world human-powered vehicle speed record of 65 miles (105 km) per hour. The driver lies flat on his or her back.

SHIMANO

Pacer 1000

BELL   Vector

LOTUS

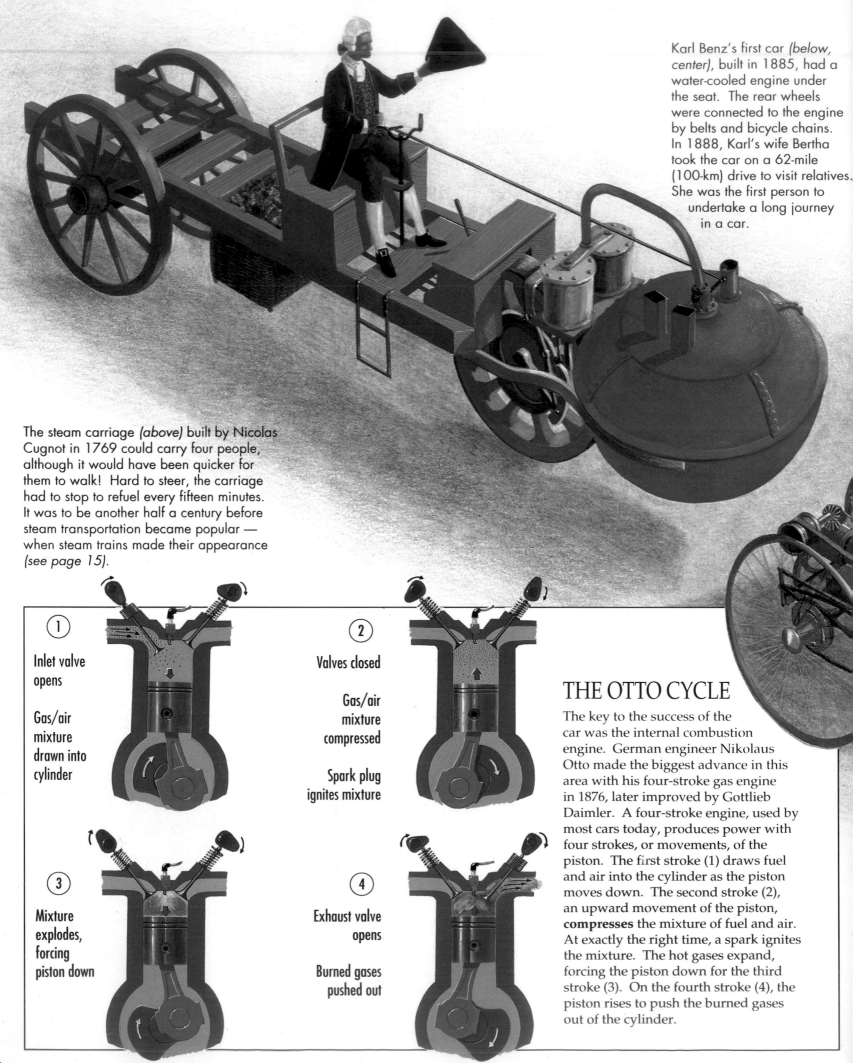

Karl Benz's first car (below, center), built in 1885, had a water-cooled engine under the seat. The rear wheels were connected to the engine by belts and bicycle chains. In 1888, Karl's wife Bertha took the car on a 62-mile (100-km) drive to visit relatives. She was the first person to undertake a long journey in a car.

The steam carriage (above) built by Nicolas Cugnot in 1769 could carry four people, although it would have been quicker for them to walk! Hard to steer, the carriage had to stop to refuel every fifteen minutes. It was to be another half a century before steam transportation became popular — when steam trains made their appearance (see page 15).

① Inlet valve opens

Gas/air mixture drawn into cylinder

② Valves closed

Gas/air mixture compressed

Spark plug ignites mixture

③ Mixture explodes, forcing piston down

④ Exhaust valve opens

Burned gases pushed out

THE OTTO CYCLE

The key to the success of the car was the internal combustion engine. German engineer Nikolaus Otto made the biggest advance in this area with his four-stroke gas engine in 1876, later improved by Gottlieb Daimler. A four-stroke engine, used by most cars today, produces power with four strokes, or movements, of the piston. The first stroke (1) draws fuel and air into the cylinder as the piston moves down. The second stroke (2), an upward movement of the piston, **compresses** the mixture of fuel and air. At exactly the right time, a spark ignites the mixture. The hot gases expand, forcing the piston down for the third stroke (3). On the fourth stroke (4), the piston rises to push the burned gases out of the cylinder.

In 1885, a few months before Benz produced his car, Gottlieb Daimler attached a gasoline engine to a wooden bicycle *(below, right)*. His son rode the world's first motor vehicle about 11 miles (17 km) around the streets of Cannstatt, Germany. During the trip, the seat, attached too close to the top of the engine, burst into flames!

THE FIRST CARS
ENTER THE HORSELESS CARRIAGE

THE FIRST SELF-PROPELLED land vehicles were powered by steam engines *(see page 12-13)*. Frenchman Nicolas Cugnot built the first steam carriage in 1769. Designed to pull heavy guns, it was in the world's first car accident when it crashed into a wall at its top speed of 3 miles (5 km) per hour!

The age of the automobile really began in 1885 when German engineer Karl Benz successfully attached a gasoline engine to a three-wheeled cycle. At first, his new car lurched and sputtered dangerously around the streets of Mannheim, but a smooth ride was soon achieved. The local newspaper reported, "Without the aid of any human element, the vehicle rolled onward, taking bends in its stride and avoiding all oncoming traffic and pedestrians. It was followed by a crowd of running and breathless youngsters."

Another German engineer, Gottlieb Daimler, invented a gasoline-powered motorcycle. Then, in 1886, he built the first four-wheeled car, a "horseless carriage" fitted with a powerful gasoline engine.

In 1890, two French machine toolmakers, René Panhard and Emile Levassor, began making cars using Daimler engines. The following year, they produced a model *(right)* that can be described as the first modern car. Fitted beneath a square hood at the front, the engine was connected to the rear wheels by a clutch and gears. Other modern devices made their first appearances in early French designs — hollow rubber tires were first used on a 1895 Peugeot; and a propeller replaced the chain drive in the first Renault built in 1898.

GOING FOR THE LAND SPEED RECORD

FROM EARLY ELECTRICS TO MODERN JETS

THE FIRST WORLD LAND SPEED RECORD was set at Achères near Paris, France, in 1898, just thirteen years after the car was invented. Count Gaston de Chasseloup-Laubat drove an electric car, the *Jeantaud*, at a speed of 39 miles (63.14 km) per hour. Medical experts at the time declared it would be impossible to breathe at those speeds and that the driver's heart would stop! Count de Chasseloup-Laubat improved on his own record a year later, to 58 miles (93.7 km) per hour. In the same year, Camille Jenatzy became the first motorist to exceed 100 km per hour. His bullet-shaped electric car, *La Jamais Contente* ("never-satisfied"), held the record for three years.

Steam-powered cars were among the early land speed record holders. One reached a speed of 74.6 miles (120 km) per hour in 1902. But they soon gave way to faster gasoline-engined cars. *Mors*, the first of the breed, broke the record in 1902. In 1927, the 300-km per hour barrier was topped by the first car specially built for the record attempt, the *Sunbeam*. This stream-lined vehicle, driven by Englishman Henry Segrave, was powered by two aircraft engines. The record was then pushed steadily higher by a series of cars with more and more powerful engines. The largest of these, *Thunderbolt*, eventually reached 345 miles (555 km) per hour in 1939.

In 1964, the gasoline engine faced new competition. Jet- and rocket-powered cars were allowed to enter the speed contest for the first time. A jet-engined car, the *Spirit of America*, took the record to over 500 miles (800 km) per hour in 1964. The first rocket-powered car, *Blue Flame*, driven by American Gary Gabelich, topped 1,000 km per hour in 1970.

The land speed racers of the early 1900s were the fastest vehicles on Earth, faster than even the primitive aircraft that were taking to the skies at the time. Racing at speeds considered fast even today, at more than 93 miles (150 km) per hour on bumpy roads, many of the drivers risked their lives.

JEANTAUD
March, 1899
58 miles (93.7 km) per hour *First electric-powered record holder*

LA JAMAIS CONTENTE
December, 1899: 66 miles (105.9 km) per hour *First record holder over 100 km per hour*

SERPOLLET
April, 1902
75 miles (120.8 km) per hour *First steam-powered record holder*

MORS
November, 1902
77 miles (124.1 km) per hour *First gasoline-powered record holder*

GOBRON-BRILLIÉ
July, 1904
103.5 miles (166.6 km) per hour *First record holder over 100 miles per hour*

BLITZEN BENZ
November, 1909
126 miles (202.7 km) per hour *First record holder over 200 km per hour*

SUNBEAM
March, 1927
203.8 miles (328 km) per hour *First record holder over 200 miles and 300 km per hour*

BLUEBIRD
February, 1932
254 miles (408.9 km) per hour *First record holder over 400 km per hour*

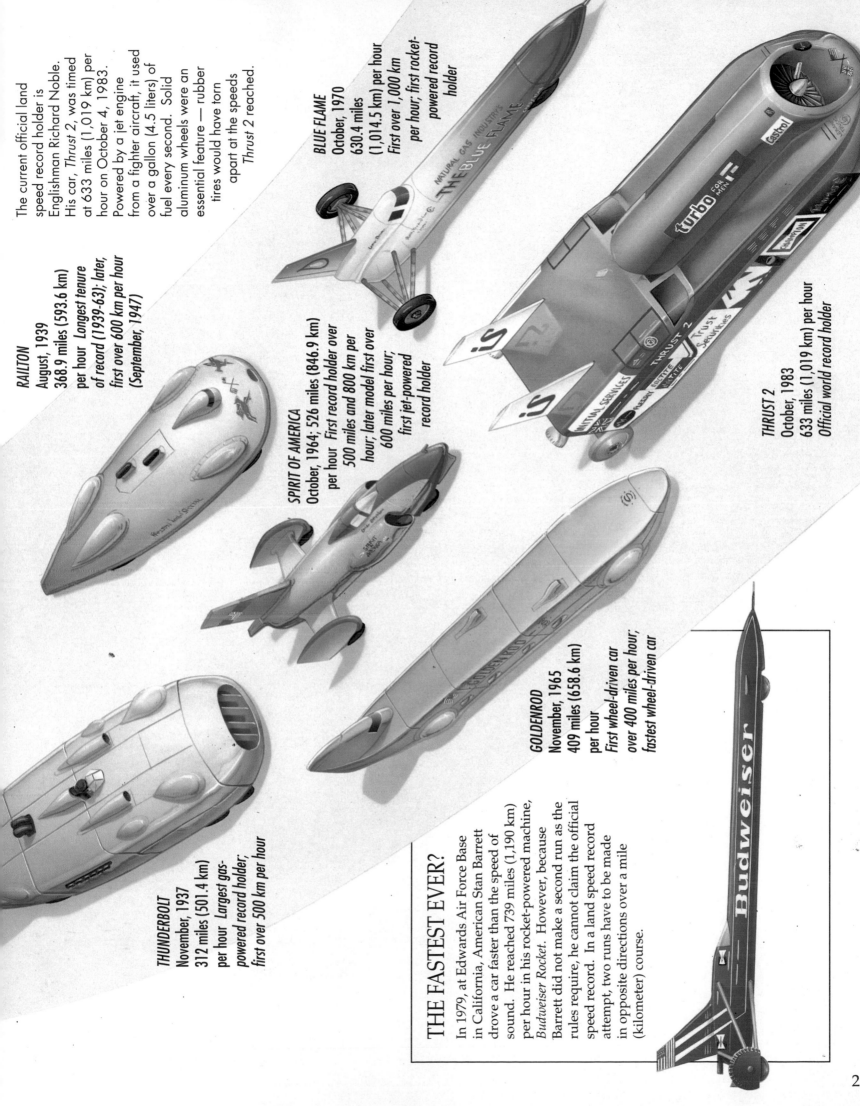

The current official land speed record holder is Englishman Richard Noble. His car, *Thrust 2*, was timed at 633 miles (1,019 km) per hour on October 4, 1983. Powered by a jet engine from a fighter aircraft, it used over a gallon (4.5 liters) of fuel every second. Solid aluminum wheels were an essential feature — rubber tires would have torn apart at the speeds *Thrust 2* reached.

BLUE FLAME
October, 1970
630.4 miles
(1,014.5 km) per hour
First over 1,000 km per hour; first rocket-powered record holder

THRUST 2
October, 1983
633 miles (1,019 km) per hour
Official world record holder

RAILTON
August, 1939
368.9 miles (593.6 km) per hour *Longest tenure of record (1939-63); later, first over 600 km per hour (September, 1947)*

SPIRIT OF AMERICA
October, 1964; 526 miles (846.9 km) per hour *First record holder over 500 miles and 800 km per hour; later model first over 600 miles per hour; first jet-powered record holder*

THUNDERBOLT
November, 1937
312 miles (501.4 km) per hour *Largest gas-powered record holder; first over 500 km per hour*

GOLDENROD
November, 1965
409 miles (658.6 km) per hour *First wheel-driven car over 400 miles per hour; fastest wheel-driven car*

THE FASTEST EVER?

In 1979, at Edwards Air Force Base in California, American Stan Barrett drove a car faster than the speed of sound. He reached 739 miles (1,190 km) per hour in his rocket-powered machine, *Budweiser Rocket*. However, because Barrett did not make a second run as the rules require, he cannot claim the official speed record. In a land speed record attempt, two runs have to be made in opposite directions over a mile (kilometer) course.

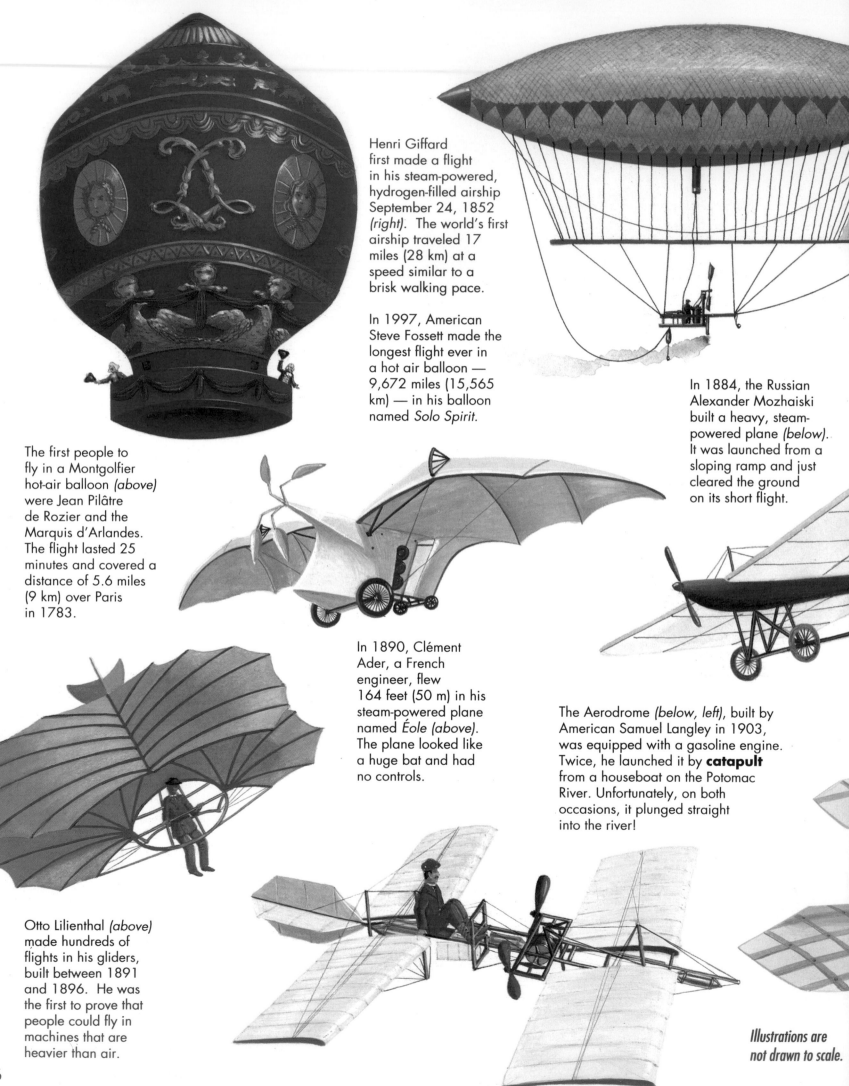

Henri Giffard first made a flight in his steam-powered, hydrogen-filled airship September 24, 1852 *(right)*. The world's first airship traveled 17 miles (28 km) at a speed similar to a brisk walking pace.

In 1997, American Steve Fossett made the longest flight ever in a hot air balloon — 9,672 miles (15,565 km) — in his balloon named *Solo Spirit*.

In 1884, the Russian Alexander Mozhaiski built a heavy, steam-powered plane *(below)*. It was launched from a sloping ramp and just cleared the ground on its short flight.

The first people to fly in a Montgolfier hot-air balloon *(above)* were Jean Pilâtre de Rozier and the Marquis d'Arlandes. The flight lasted 25 minutes and covered a distance of 5.6 miles (9 km) over Paris in 1783.

In 1890, Clément Ader, a French engineer, flew 164 feet (50 m) in his steam-powered plane named *Éole (above)*. The plane looked like a huge bat and had no controls.

The Aerodrome *(below, left)*, built by American Samuel Langley in 1903, was equipped with a gasoline engine. Twice, he launched it by **catapult** from a houseboat on the Potomac River. Unfortunately, on both occasions, it plunged straight into the river!

Otto Lilienthal *(above)* made hundreds of flights in his gliders, built between 1891 and 1896. He was the first to prove that people could fly in machines that are heavier than air.

Illustrations are not drawn to scale.

THE FIRST AIRCRAFT
THE QUEST FOR FLIGHT

In 1849, a glider built by George Cayley (right) was launched from a hillside with a ten-year-old boy on board. It flew about 1,641 feet (500 m).

Félix du Temple built the first powered airplane in 1857. A full-sized, steam-powered plane (right) took off from a steep ramp seventeen years later. This was the first-known flight by a piloted, powered airplane.

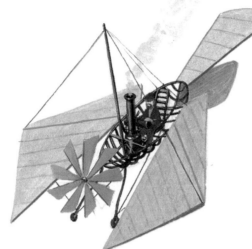

THE FIRST SUCCESSFUL flying machines were balloons filled with hot air. A hot-air balloon was launched on June 15, 1783, by two French brothers, Joseph and Etienne Montgolfier. It rose to a height of about 5,906 feet (1,800 m). Later that year, they demonstrated their invention to the king and queen of France. This time, the balloon carried three animals. After a short flight, the animals landed safely. On November 21, 1783, the first human passengers, Jean Pilâtre de Rozier and the Marquis d'Arlandes, braved a flight in a Montgolfier balloon. They were the first aviators in history.

It was Englishman George Cayley who designed the modern airplane, with wings and a tail like those flying today. However, none of his machines ever flew for long — in the mid-nineteenth century, no engine yet invented was light enough to power a piloted flying machine.

The first people to put a gasoline engine on an airplane and achieve a controlled flight were the American brothers, Wilbur and Orville Wright. Their aircraft, *Flyer I,* was first launched on December 17, 1903.

Karl Jatho of Germany was close to claiming the record for the first flight. Although it lacked controls, his kite-like airplane (left) made flights at distances up to 197 feet (60 m).

FIRST CONTROLLED, POWERED FLIGHT

The historic first flight of the Wright brothers' *Flyer I (above)* took place on sand dunes near Kitty Hawk, North Carolina. With Orville at the controls, *Flyer I* remained aloft about twelve seconds and flew a distance of just 118 feet (36 m), less than the wingspan of many modern airliners. By changing the angle of the wingtips, or warping, the Wrights could control their aircraft. Theirs was the first controlled, powered flight.

THE FIRST HELICOPTERS
FROM FLYING TOP TO SIKORSKY

THE WAY IN WHICH a helicopter flies has been understood for many centuries. For example, a flying top was invented by the Chinese in about 500 B.C. It was a small propeller that flew upward when the stick on which it was balanced was rapidly spun. The propeller "bit" into the air, producing **uplift**. This method of flight worked well for small toys, but how could a machine capable of carrying people through the air be built? Only when lightweight gasoline engines *(see page 22)* became available in the early 1900s could the helicopter take to the skies.

The first flight by a piloted helicopter was achieved in 1907 by Frenchman Paul Cornu. However, he and other early helicopter pilots were not yet able to control their machines. The helicopters twisted in the opposite direction of the blades when the aircraft moved forward. The German aircraft designer Heinrich Focke and Russian-born American engineer Igor Sikorsky came up with the answer. They solved the problem by using two parts called **rotors**, each one turning in opposite directions.

A FLYING TOP

Leonardo da Vinci, Italian painter, scientist, and engineer, was fascinated with the idea of helicopter flight. His design, produced in about 1500, had a corkscrew-shaped rotor which, he thought, would soar upward through the air as it spun. To power the machine, the pilot pulled sharply on a rope wound around a central column — similar to operating a Chinese flying top. But da Vinci's machine never flew. He was, however, the first person to use the word *helicopter* from the Greek words meaning "spiral wing."

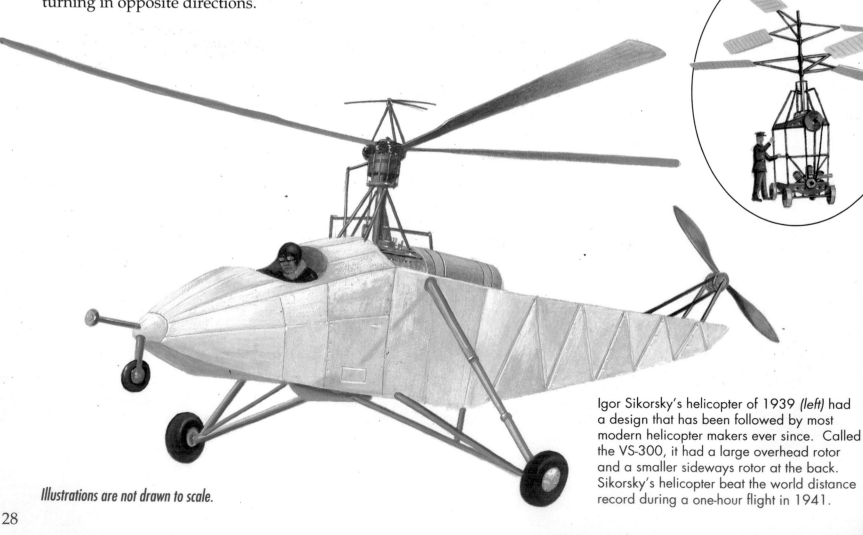

Illustrations are not drawn to scale.

Igor Sikorsky's helicopter of 1939 *(left)* had a design that has been followed by most modern helicopter makers ever since. Called the VS-300, it had a large overhead rotor and a smaller sideways rotor at the back. Sikorsky's helicopter beat the world distance record during a one-hour flight in 1941.

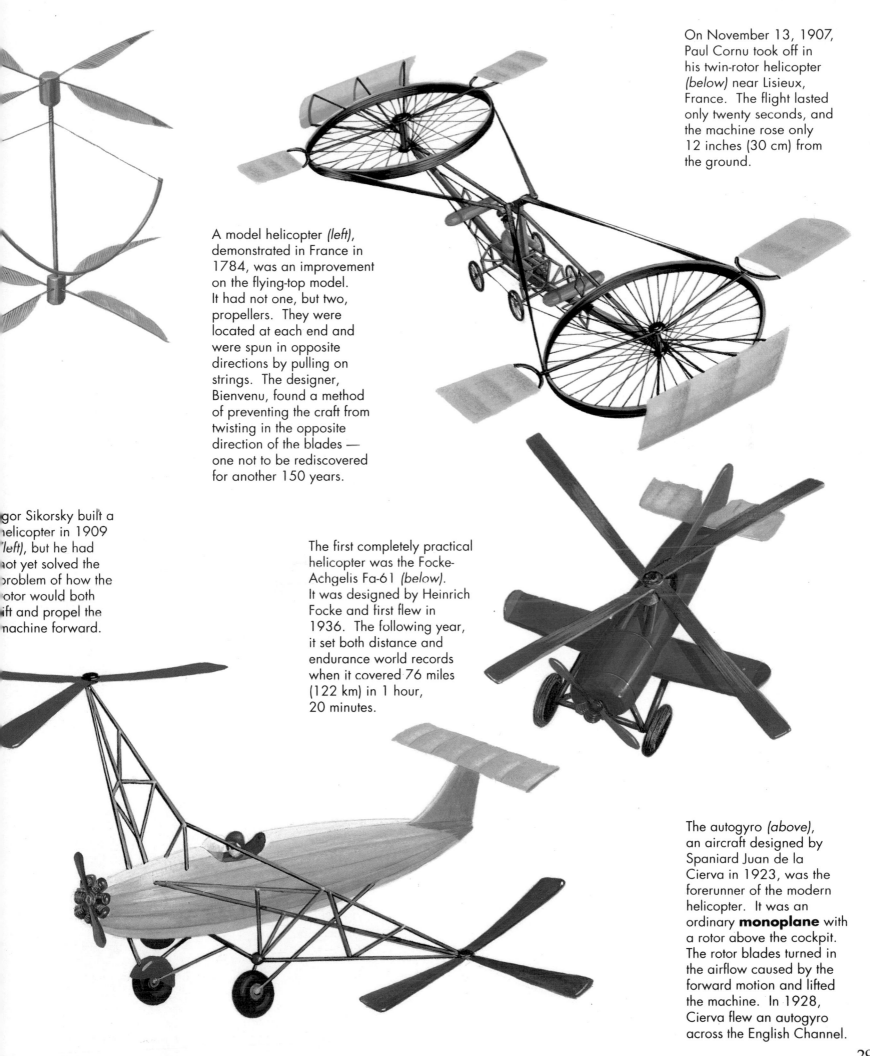

A model helicopter *(left)*, demonstrated in France in 1784, was an improvement on the flying-top model. It had not one, but two, propellers. They were located at each end and were spun in opposite directions by pulling on strings. The designer, Bienvenu, found a method of preventing the craft from twisting in the opposite direction of the blades — one not to be rediscovered for another 150 years.

gor Sikorsky built a helicopter in 1909 *(left)*, but he had not yet solved the problem of how the rotor would both lift and propel the machine forward.

The first completely practical helicopter was the Focke-Achgelis Fa-61 *(below)*. It was designed by Heinrich Focke and first flew in 1936. The following year, it set both distance and endurance world records when it covered 76 miles (122 km) in 1 hour, 20 minutes.

The autogyro *(above)*, an aircraft designed by Spaniard Juan de la Cierva in 1923, was the forerunner of the modern helicopter. It was an ordinary **monoplane** with a rotor above the cockpit. The rotor blades turned in the airflow caused by the forward motion and lifted the machine. In 1928, Cierva flew an autogyro across the English Channel.

THE FLIGHT OF THE *SPIRIT OF ST. LOUIS*

CHARLES LINDBERGH was the first person to fly solo across the Atlantic Ocean, but he was not the first to cross it nonstop by air. On June 14-15, 1919, British pilots Captain John Alcock and Lieutenant Arthur Whitten Brown flew a Vickers Vimy bomber from St. John's, Newfoundland, to County Galway in Ireland in 16 hours, 27 minutes.

In 1926, New York hotel owner Raymond Orteig offered a $25,000 prize to anyone who could fly non-stop from New York to Paris. The following year, Lindbergh, a twenty-five-year-old chief pilot for an air-mail company, could not resist the challenge. He decided he would need a new plane, specially built for the journey. It would be a monoplane, capable of carrying the 450 gallons (1,700 liters) of fuel he needed for the journey. He also made up his mind it would be a solo flight.

Early in the day on May 19, 1927, the *Spirit of St. Louis*, loaded down with fuel and barely able to leave the ground, took off from Roosevelt Field, New York. It just cleared the telegraph wires at the end of the runway.

The cockpit had side windows but no forward view at all, although there was a **periscope**.

NEW YORK

Lindbergh navigated by measuring how far he had traveled in a certain direction (dead reckoning), while guessing the wind simply from looking at the waves below! The flight was full of dangers. As Lindbergh struggled to remain awake, ice forming on the wings threatened to down his airplane. Several times the *Spirit of St. Louis* almost brushed the waves as its pilot flew low to avoid fog. Lindbergh was not always sure he was on course.

After twenty-eight hours, however, Lindbergh found himself flying over Valentia Island, southwest of Ireland. To his disbelief, he realized he was only 3 miles (5 km) off course. Six hours later, he landed in Paris to a hero's welcome. The *Spirit of St. Louis* had crossed the Atlantic Ocean from New York to Paris — a distance of 3,616 miles (5,819 km) — in 33 hours, 30 minutes. And Lindbergh had done it solo.

FIRST SOLO TRANSATLANTIC FLIGHT
LINDBERGH'S FAMOUS JOURNEY

Spirit of St.Louis

PARIS

THE FASTEST JET AIRCRAFT
LOCKHEED SR-71 — BLACKBIRD

THE FASTEST JET AIRCRAFT ever to have flown was an American spy plane, the Lockheed SR-71. Known as Blackbird because of its sleek, black appearance, it was designed to fly fast and high over enemy territory, photographing military bases. From a height of over 15 miles (25 km), Blackbird's powerful cameras could take a clear shot of a car license plate!

Blackbird's top speed was 2,430 miles (3,911 km) per hour — about three times the speed of sound. Its two engines produced more power than those of a large ocean liner. On September 1, 1974, it made the fastest-ever flight across the Atlantic Ocean, crossing from New York to London in just under 1 hour, 55 minutes (a normal airliner takes about seven hours).

The Lockheed SR-71 was taken out of service in 1990. Some military experts think the U.S. Air Force may be developing an even faster jet. Called Aurora, it may be capable of flying 18.6 miles (30 km) high at twice Blackbird's speed!

Illustrations are approximately to scale.

The first aircraft to fly faster than sound was a rocket-powered airplane named *Glamorous Glennis*. On October 14, 1947, Chuck Yeager of the U.S. Air Force flew the X-1, as it was officially known, at a speed of 700 miles (1,126 km) per hour above the Mojave Desert in California.

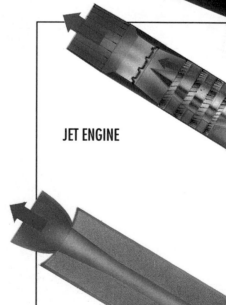

JET ENGINE

ROCKET ENGINE

FASTEST OF ALL

On October 3, 1967, U.S. pilot William Knight flew a rocket-powered plane at a speed of 4,520 miles (7,274 km) per hour — nearly seven times the speed of sound. This aircraft, the X-15 (left), could not take off from the ground and was carried aloft underneath a large transporter plane. When the transporter reached its maximum altitude, the X-15's rocket engines ignited and blasted away to the record.

As thin as an aluminum can, the outer walls of the Blackbird were painted with a special heat-radiating black paint that could withstand temperatures of over 572°F (300°C). The Blackbird experienced these temperatures as it traveled at high speeds. When it sped along, the plane grew 32 inches (80 cm) in length as the metal expanded.

Like Blackbird, the X-15 was built to withstand high temperatures generated at high speeds. Its outer walls became fourteen times hotter than boiling water during flight.

The X-15 holds more than one record. Unlike jet engines, its rocket-powered engines did not need air to run. So the X-15 could fly much higher than jet aircraft, to levels of the atmosphere where the air is very thin. On August 22, 1963, the X-15 reached an altitude of 354,217 feet (107,960 m), a record altitude for any aircraft.

JETS AND ROCKETS

In a jet engine, air enters a compressor, or fan, at its front end. The fan compresses the air and feeds it through to the combustion chamber. There, fuel is sprayed in, and the mixture is ignited. The hot gas produced expands and blasts out at the rear of the engine. The gases streaming backward push the aircraft forward.

A rocket, on the other hand, can operate in outer space where there is no air. In a solid fuel rocket engine, fuel burns rapidly, producing a large amount of hot gas. The gas blasts from the rear of the rocket, driving the craft forward, just as with a jet engine.

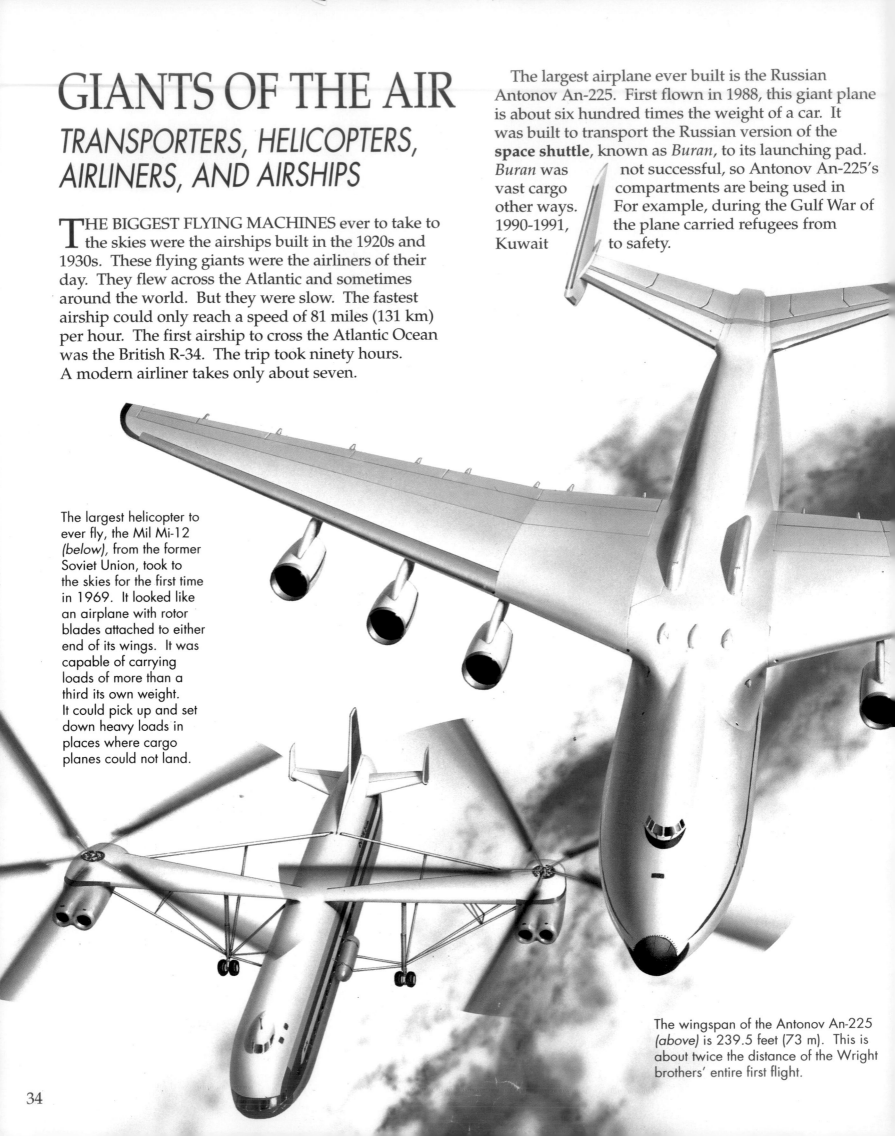

GIANTS OF THE AIR
TRANSPORTERS, HELICOPTERS, AIRLINERS, AND AIRSHIPS

THE BIGGEST FLYING MACHINES ever to take to the skies were the airships built in the 1920s and 1930s. These flying giants were the airliners of their day. They flew across the Atlantic and sometimes around the world. But they were slow. The fastest airship could only reach a speed of 81 miles (131 km) per hour. The first airship to cross the Atlantic Ocean was the British R-34. The trip took ninety hours. A modern airliner takes only about seven.

The largest airplane ever built is the Russian Antonov An-225. First flown in 1988, this giant plane is about six hundred times the weight of a car. It was built to transport the Russian version of the **space shuttle**, known as *Buran*, to its launching pad. *Buran* was not successful, so Antonov An-225's vast cargo compartments are being used in other ways. For example, during the Gulf War of 1990-1991, the plane carried refugees from Kuwait to safety.

The largest helicopter to ever fly, the Mil Mi-12 *(below),* from the former Soviet Union, took to the skies for the first time in 1969. It looked like an airplane with rotor blades attached to either end of its wings. It was capable of carrying loads of more than a third its own weight. It could pick up and set down heavy loads in places where cargo planes could not land.

The wingspan of the Antonov An-225 *(above)* is 239.5 feet (73 m). This is about twice the distance of the Wright brothers' entire first flight.

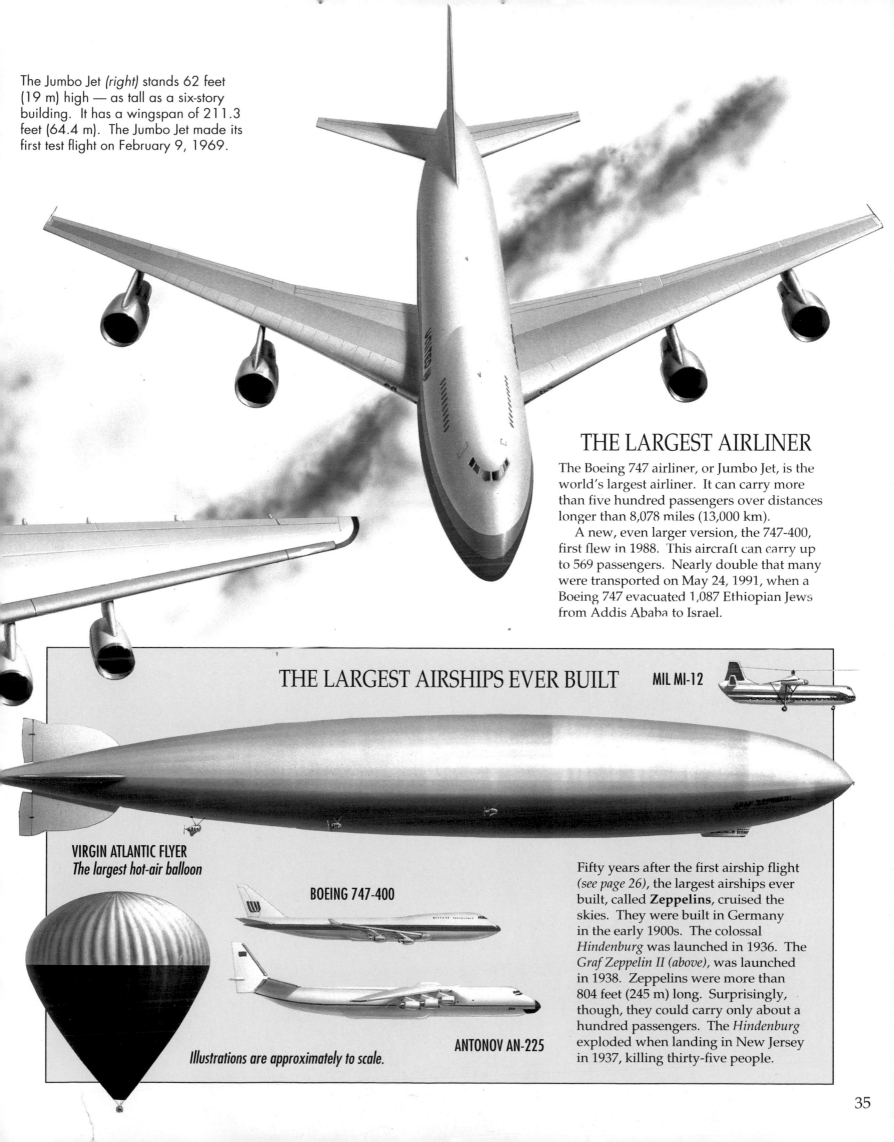

The Jumbo Jet *(right)* stands 62 feet (19 m) high — as tall as a six-story building. It has a wingspan of 211.3 feet (64.4 m). The Jumbo Jet made its first test flight on February 9, 1969.

THE LARGEST AIRLINER

The Boeing 747 airliner, or Jumbo Jet, is the world's largest airliner. It can carry more than five hundred passengers over distances longer than 8,078 miles (13,000 km).

A new, even larger version, the 747-400, first flew in 1988. This aircraft can carry up to 569 passengers. Nearly double that many were transported on May 24, 1991, when a Boeing 747 evacuated 1,087 Ethiopian Jews from Addis Ababa to Israel.

THE LARGEST AIRSHIPS EVER BUILT   MIL MI-12

VIRGIN ATLANTIC FLYER
The largest hot-air balloon

BOEING 747-400

ANTONOV AN-225

Illustrations are approximately to scale.

Fifty years after the first airship flight *(see page 26)*, the largest airships ever built, called **Zeppelins**, cruised the skies. They were built in Germany in the early 1900s. The colossal *Hindenburg* was launched in 1936. The *Graf Zeppelin II (above)*, was launched in 1938. Zeppelins were more than 804 feet (245 m) long. Surprisingly, though, they could carry only about a hundred passengers. The *Hindenburg* exploded when landing in New Jersey in 1937, killing thirty-five people.

Command
Module

Lunar
Module

Third stage

Second stage

THE LARGEST ROCKET

AND FAMOUS FIRSTS IN SPACE TECHNOLOGY

To REACH OUTER SPACE, a vehicle must overcome the pull of Earth's gravity. It must reach a speed of at least 17,710 miles (28,500 km) per hour. Only immensely powerful rockets (*see page 33*) can achieve such speeds.

The first rockets, built by American scientist Robert Goddard in 1926, were only 3 feet (1 m) tall. The *Vostok* rocket that put the first **satellite** in orbit more than thirty years later was 115 feet (35 m) tall. The Apollo astronauts were carried into space on their way to the Moon in 1969 in a *Saturn V*. The 364-foot (111-m) rocket was the largest ever built. The open-style building that housed *Saturn V* was so vast that a special air-conditioning system was needed to stop clouds from forming and rain from falling inside!

Saturn V was fifty times as powerful as a Boeing 747 jumbo jet. The most powerful rocket today is the Russian *Energia*. Its four engines are capable of carrying a load as heavy as twenty-four family cars into orbit. Its original purpose was to launch a space shuttle and perhaps even to send a spaceship to Mars.

Illustrations are approximately to scale.

INSIDE SATURN V

Saturn V (right), like all launch vehicles, is made from several separate rockets, or stages, joined together. The first rocket is at the bottom and lifts the other stages into the air. When that first rocket runs out of fuel, it drops to the ground. Then the second stage rocket fires. The second stage, too, falls away when its fuel is gone. Then the third stage fires and lifts the spacecraft into orbit. In this illustration, the Apollo Command and Lunar modules are launched.

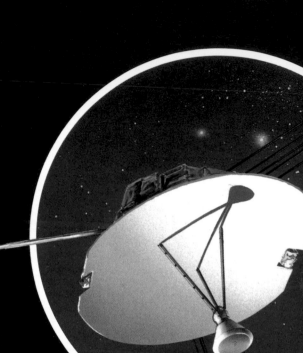

PIONEER 10

SPACE PIONEER

In January, 1993, the U.S. space probe *Pioneer 10 (right)* was 5.3 billion miles (8.5 billion km) from Earth. Even at that distance, its radio signal can still be picked up on Earth by powerful receivers. *Pioneer 10* carries a plaque showing where it came from in case intelligent life from elsewhere finds it. The probe is the most distant human-made object from Earth. Its record will one day be beaten by another space probe, *Voyager 1*.

Liquid
kerosene
tank

Liquid
oxygen
tank

First stage

The U.S. space shuttle *Columbia (left)* became the world's first reused spacecraft when it made its second flight in November, 1981. Its first flight was earlier that year.

NASA

The Soviet *Vostok* rocket *(below)* carried the first **artificial satellite** into orbit. Called *Sputnik 1 (close-up, below left)*, it was launched October 4, 1957, and remained in orbit ninety-two days.

The first-ever rocket *(below, left)* was launched March 16, 1926, by American Robert Goddard. It used liquid gases for fuel and reached a height of 41 feet (12.5 m).

The first long-range liquid-fuel rocket was the German V2 *(below, right)*, built in 1942. It was 46 feet (14 m) long and had a range of 199 miles (320 km).

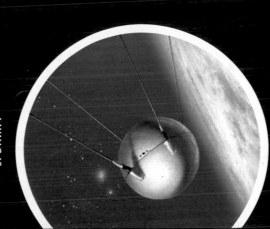

SPUTNIK 1

V2
ROCKET

GODDARD'S
ROCKET

FIRST TO THE MOON
THE FLIGHT OF APOLLO 11

THE FIRST LANDING by a piloted spacecraft on another body in our Solar System took place July 20, 1969, when *Apollo 11* touched down on the surface of the Moon. A few hours later, U.S. astronaut Neil Armstrong became the first person to step onto the lunar surface.

The spacecraft that took Armstrong and his fellow astronauts Edwin Aldrin and Michael Collins to the Moon was built in several sections, each with a different function. The Command Module (CM), located in the nose of *Apollo 11*, was both the control center and cramped living quarters for the crew. The Service Module (SM) contained the main rocket engine that powered the spacecraft. The Lunar Module (LM) was in two parts — both descended to the Moon itself, but only the upper section lifted off again.

Five more moon landings followed, the last in 1972. The Apollo astronauts collected 838 pounds (380 kilograms) of rocks and soil from six different locations. The rocks and soil are important in the study of the Moon and may give scientists information about the origins of Earth, as well.

Astronauts Armstrong and Aldrin spent 2½ hours gathering rock and soil samples from the Moon. They were watched by millions of television viewers. Footprints they left behind will last for ten million years.

MOON LANDING
Once *Apollo 11* was in orbit around the Moon, one astronaut stayed in the CSM. The other two moved into the LM. The LM separated from the CSM (4) and descended to the Moon (5).

38

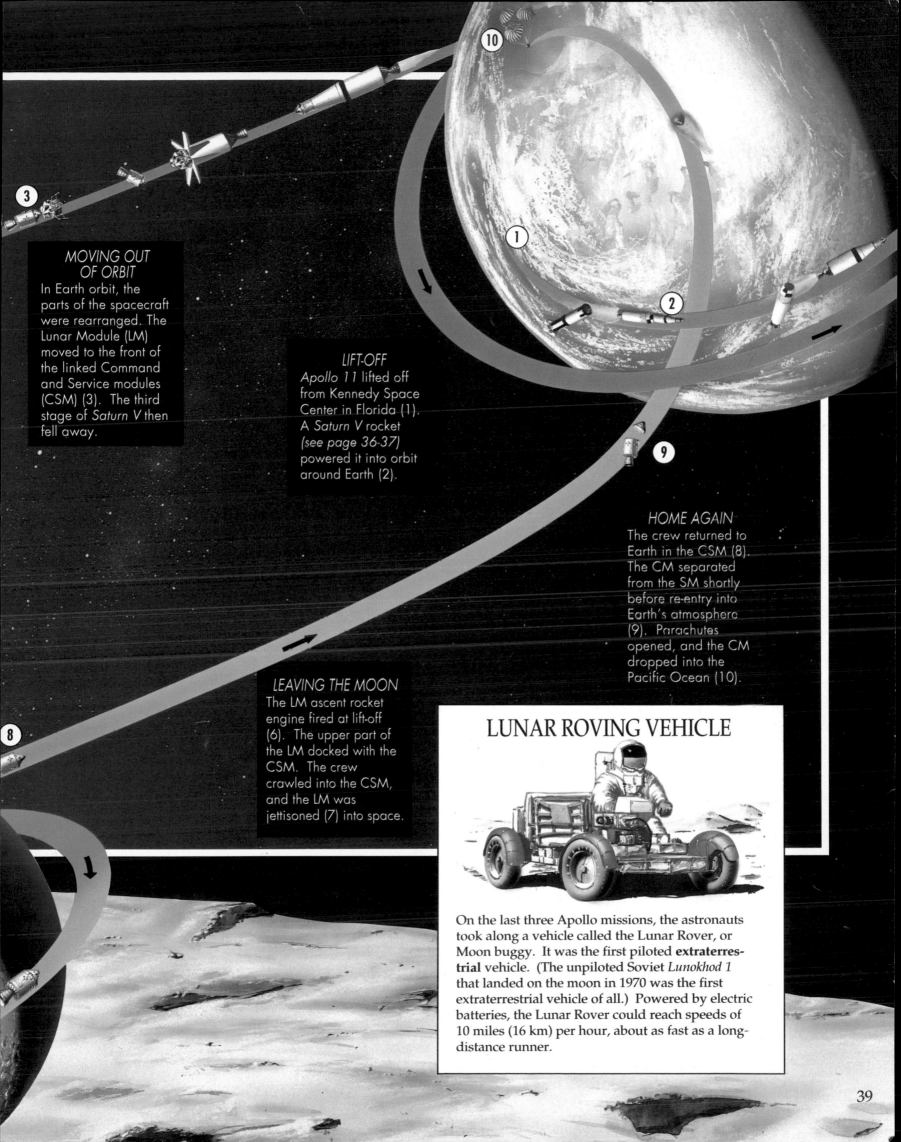

MOVING OUT OF ORBIT
In Earth orbit, the parts of the spacecraft were rearranged. The Lunar Module (LM) moved to the front of the linked Command and Service modules (CSM) (3). The third stage of *Saturn V* then fell away.

LIFT-OFF
Apollo 11 lifted off from Kennedy Space Center in Florida (1). A *Saturn V* rocket *(see page 36-37)* powered it into orbit around Earth (2).

HOME AGAIN
The crew returned to Earth in the CSM (8). The CM separated from the SM shortly before re-entry into Earth's atmosphere (9). Parachutes opened, and the CM dropped into the Pacific Ocean (10).

LEAVING THE MOON
The LM ascent rocket engine fired at lift-off (6). The upper part of the LM docked with the CSM. The crew crawled into the CSM, and the LM was jettisoned (7) into space.

LUNAR ROVING VEHICLE

On the last three Apollo missions, the astronauts took along a vehicle called the Lunar Rover, or Moon buggy. It was the first piloted **extraterrestrial** vehicle. (The unpiloted Soviet *Lunokhod 1* that landed on the moon in 1970 was the first extraterrestrial vehicle of all.) Powered by electric batteries, the Lunar Rover could reach speeds of 10 miles (16 km) per hour, about as fast as a long-distance runner.

HIGH FLYERS

HIGH-ALTITUDE RECORD HOLDERS

MANY OF THE STARS in the sky are so far away that their distances are measured in *light-years*. One light-year is the distance traveled by light, moving at 186,290 miles (299,792 km) per second, in one year. Even the nearest star (except for the Sun) is more than 4 light-years away. The farthest object ever detected by Earth-based technology may be more than 13 *billion* light-years away!

By comparison, the greatest efforts made by humans to lift themselves clear of their home planet seem tiny. The altitude record is held by the crew of *Apollo 13*, whose spacecraft reached a distance of just over 248,560 miles (400,000 km) from Earth on April 15, 1970. This was, however, a major advance over the first-ever piloted space flight made by Yuri Gagarin, whose Soviet *Vostok I* spacecraft climbed to an altitude of just 203 miles (327 km) nine years earlier.

Apart from spacecraft, the champion high-flyer is the U.S. rocket-powered plane X-15, also famous for its speed records *(see page 33)*. It flew so high — more than 328,100 feet (100,000 m) — that its pilot was able to qualify as an astronaut! Jet-powered planes cannot ascend to such heights because they need air for their engines to operate. A MiG fighter jet holds the altitude record at 123,530 feet (37,650 m).

HIGHEST IN A BALLOON

The greatest height ever reached by a piloted balloon is 123,809 feet (37,735 m). This record was achieved by Nicholas Piantanida in South Dakota in February, 1966. Unfortunately, Piantanida did not survive the feat, and his achievement is not recognized as a record.

The official altitude record is, therefore still held by U.S. Navy officers Malcolm Ross and Victor Prather. Their elongated balloon *Lee Lewis Memorial* rose to 113,746 feet (34,668 m) in 1961.

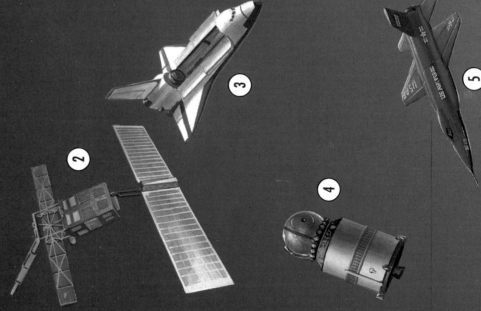

The all-time altitude record is held by the U.S. astronauts aboard *Apollo 13*. The spacecraft was to land on the Moon, but an explosion scrapped the Moon mission. The craft orbited the Moon and returned to Earth.

MOON
238,866 miles
(384,400 km)

MT. EVEREST *Highest mountain*
29,080 feet (8,863 m)

1 *Apollo 13 Farthest piloted flight* 1970 248,676 miles (400,187 km)
2 Satellite 22,370 miles (36,000 km)
3 Space shuttle
4 *Vostok 1 First piloted space flight* 1961 203 miles (327 km)
5 *X-15 Highest flight by aircraft* 1963 354,217 feet (107,960 m)
6 *MiG 25 Highest flight by jet aircraft* 1977 123,530 feet (37,650 m)
7 *Lee Lewis Memorial Highest flight by balloon* 1961
113,746 feet (34,668 m)
8 Lockheed SR-71 *Blackbird* 98,430 feet (30,000 m)
9 Concorde 59,058 feet (18,000 m)
10 *Aérospatiale SA315b Lama Highest flight by helicopter* 1972
40,822 feet (12,442 m)
11 Boeing 747 32,810 feet (10,000 m)

Illustrations are not drawn to scale.

41

HUBBLE SPACE TELESCOPE
GIANT STAR WATCHER IN ORBIT

THE BEST TELESCOPES in the world all suffer from one thing — the air they must "see" through is polluted and tends to move. Because of this, the more distant stars appear faint or blurred, even if **observatories** are located on mountaintops far away from city lights and smog. Therefore, for the best views, telescopes need to be located above Earth's atmosphere. That is exactly where the most powerful of them all, the Hubble Space Telescope, is to be found — orbiting 383 miles (616 km) above Earth.

Like most large, modern telescopes, the Hubble is a **reflecting telescope** — it uses mirrors to focus an image of the stars or galaxies. The Hubble allows astronomers to clearly see stars fifty times fainter and ten times farther away than they could using any of the best telescopes on the ground. The Hubble Space Telescope is so powerful, it could detect light from a tiny flashlight over 248,560 miles (400,000 km) away.

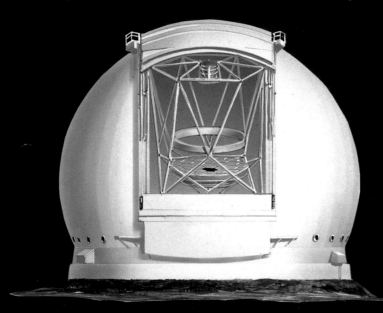

THE HONEYCOMB TELESCOPE

The Keck telescope, sitting atop the 13,780-foot (4,200-m) peak of Mauna Kea on Hawaii, is the world's largest telescope. Its light-collecting mirror, measuring 33 feet (10 m) across, consists of thirty-six **hexagons**. This is almost twice as large as a mirror in the world's next-largest telescope, the 200-inch (508-cm) Hale telescope at Mount Palomar, California. The Keck telescope is so sensitive that it could detect a candle shining more than 62,140 miles (100,000 km) away.

INSIDE THE HUBBLE
The main mirror (1) reflects light from distant stars and galaxies onto the secondary mirror (2). This focuses the light down through a central tube (3) to detectors (4). A television image can be transmitted to Earth using the antennae (5). Computers redirect the telescope. Solar panels (6) turn sunlight into electric power for the telescope.

THE FIRST STARGAZER

In 1609, Italian scientist Galileo became the first person to gaze at the night sky through a telescope. To his amazement, he saw that the Moon had mountains and craters, and that the planet Jupiter had several moons circling it. He also discovered many new stars never before seen by humans.

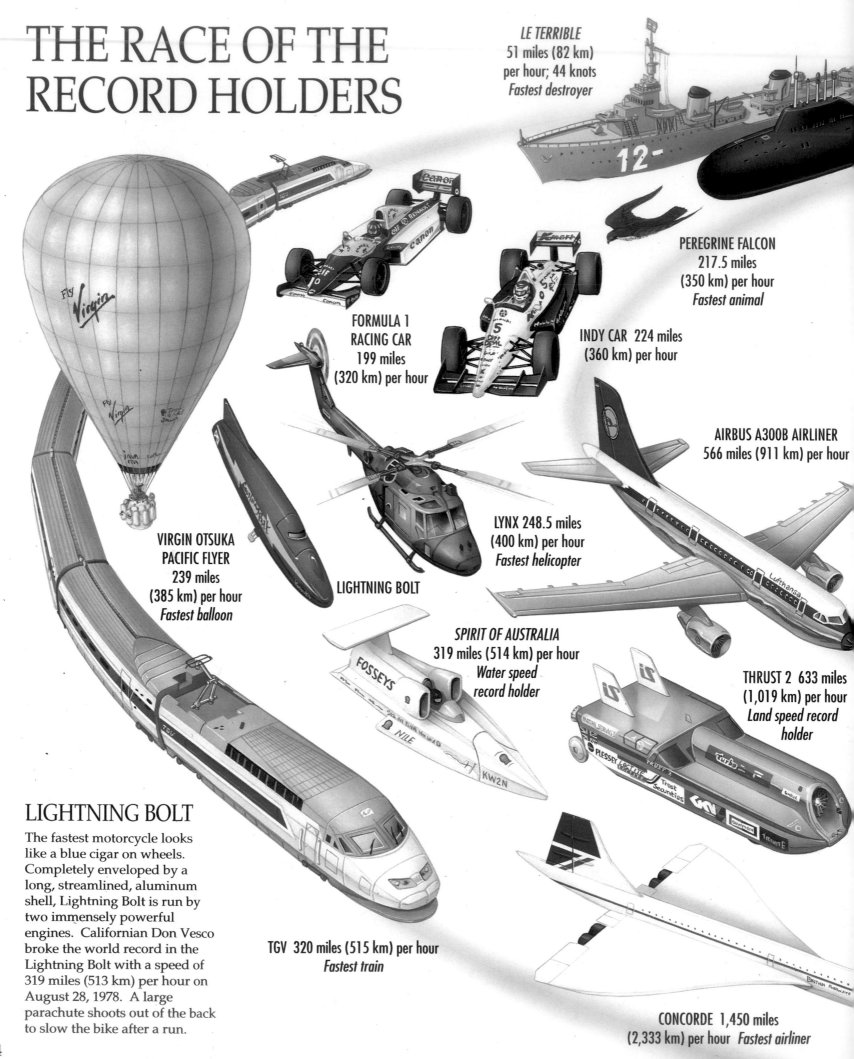

THE RACE OF THE RECORD HOLDERS

LE TERRIBLE
51 miles (82 km)
per hour; 44 knots
Fastest destroyer

PEREGRINE FALCON
217.5 miles
(350 km) per hour
Fastest animal

**FORMULA 1
RACING CAR**
199 miles
(320 km) per hour

INDY CAR 224 miles
(360 km) per hour

AIRBUS A300B AIRLINER
566 miles (911 km) per hour

**VIRGIN OTSUKA
PACIFIC FLYER**
239 miles
(385 km) per hour
Fastest balloon

LIGHTNING BOLT

LYNX 248.5 miles
(400 km) per hour
Fastest helicopter

SPIRIT OF AUSTRALIA
319 miles (514 km) per hour
*Water speed
record holder*

THRUST 2 633 miles
(1,019 km) per hour
*Land speed record
holder*

LIGHTNING BOLT

The fastest motorcycle looks
like a blue cigar on wheels.
Completely enveloped by a
long, streamlined, aluminum
shell, Lightning Bolt is run by
two immensely powerful
engines. Californian Don Vesco
broke the world record in the
Lightning Bolt with a speed of
319 miles (513 km) per hour on
August 28, 1978. A large
parachute shoots out of the back
to slow the bike after a run.

TGV 320 miles (515 km) per hour
Fastest train

CONCORDE 1,450 miles
(2,333 km) per hour *Fastest airliner*

RACING BICYCLE
45 miles (72 km) per hour

RACEHORSE 43 miles
(69 km) per hour

UNITED STATES
41 miles (66 km)
per hour; 36 knots
Fastest ocean liner

J CLASS RACING YACHT 35 miles (56 km) per hour; 30 knots

THERMOPYLAE 24 miles (39 km) per hour
One of the fastest clippers

ALFA CLASS SUBMARINE
miles (82 km) per hour; 44 knots
Fastest submarine

THE GREATEST SPEEDS achieved by human-made machines have all been reached in space, where there is no air to slow objects down. Even a satellite orbits Earth at twice the speed of Earth's fastest aircraft. The unpiloted space probe *Helios B*, sent to observe the Sun, holds the all-time speed record of 157,090 miles (252,800 km) per hour. A spacecraft moving at that speed could travel from Earth to the Moon in an hour and a half! The crew of *Apollo 10* (U.S. astronauts Thomas Stafford, Eugene Cernan, and John Young) holds the record for the fastest speed at which humans have traveled. The crew accomplished this when their command module returned to Earth from the Moon on May 26, 1969.

Illustrations are not drawn to scale.

One hundred fifty years ago, large sailing ships called clippers *(above)* vied with each other to be the quickest on the high seas. Loaded with tea and powered only by the wind, the clippers raced nonstop from China to Europe — more than halfway around the world — in about a hundred days. But sea-going speed champions are generally fairly slow when compared to other fields. A clipper never went faster than a human sprinter. And both a modern racing yacht and the fastest ocean liner (the *United States*) would be left behind by a racehorse. Only the quickest warships and submarines can outpace a racing cyclist, and any family car could easily overtake them all.

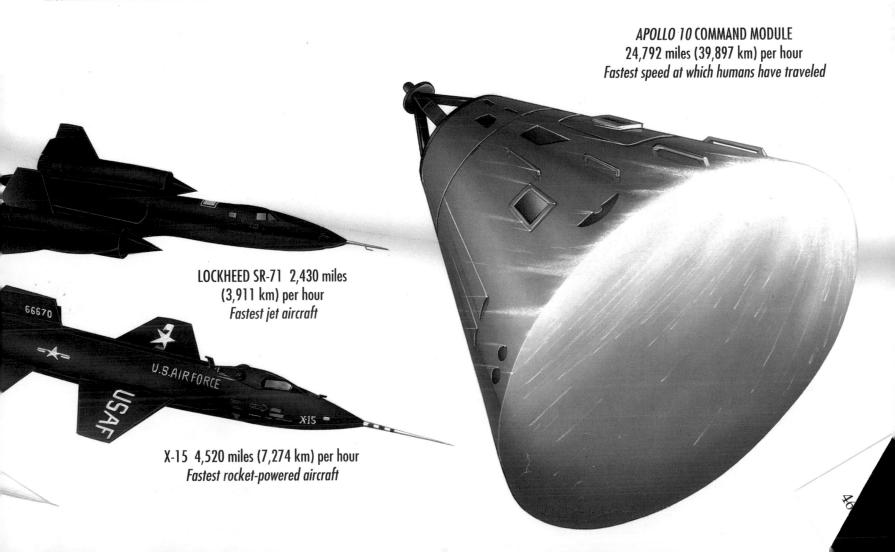

APOLLO 10 **COMMAND MODULE**
24,792 miles (39,897 km) per hour
Fastest speed at which humans have traveled

LOCKHEED SR-71 2,430 miles
(3,911 km) per hour
Fastest jet aircraft

66670

U.S. AIR FORCE

USAF

X-15

X-15 4,520 miles (7,274 km) per hour
Fastest rocket-powered aircraft

GLOSSARY

artificial satellite — a human-made object sent into space that orbits a body in space, such as a planet.

atmospheric pressure — the weight of the air on objects at sea level.

catapult *(v)* — to throw or launch into the air with a device made for that purpose.

compresses *(v)* — squeezes or presses together into a smaller space.

condensed — changed from a gas into either a liquid or solid form.

daguerreotype — an early photograph produced on a silver or silver-covered copper plate. The process was invented by Louis Daguerre.

extraterrestrial — originating or living outside of Earth or its atmosphere.

hexagon — a shape with six angles and six sides.

light-year — the distance light travels through space in a year.

magnetic levitation — the scientific principle by which powerful magnets attached to a track push away another set of powerful magnets attached to an object, such as a train. The result is the object moves forward while being suspended above the track.

monoplane — an airplane that has just one pair of wings.

observatories — structures designed and equipped to study space, including the stars, the planets, and the weather.

periscope — an optical instrument that contains mirrors or prisms that can observe objects from behind obstructions.

propeller — a device with blades that is rotated by an engine. The propeller propels an object, such as a boat or plane, forward.

reflecting telescope — a scientific instrument that uses one or more mirrors as the principal means of focusing so that distant objects can be viewed up close.

rotors — parts of a machine that rotate.

satellite — an object, artificial or natural (a moon), that orbits a body in space, such as a planet.

seismograph — a device that detects and records the activity of earthquakes.

space shuttle — a reusable space vehicle that is designed to carry astronauts between Earth and space stations.

uplift — a force that causes an object to be lifted off the ground.

vacuum — a space that does not contain air.

Zeppelin — a rigid airship that is in the shape of a cylinder.

RESEARCH PROJECTS

1. An instant camera can produce a photograph in just a few seconds. Find out what processes make instant photography possible. Trace the history of instant photography from its early black-and-white stages to color photography.

2. Find some information at the library or on the World Wide Web about the luxury ocean liner, the *Titanic*, and the airship, the *Hindenburg*. Do some research to discover how these mighty ships met their tragic ends.

3. Trace the development of the clock from Yi Xing's mechanical clock in A.D. 725 to today's state-of-the-art, battery-powered wristwatches.

4. What type of transportation fascinates you most — the automobile, the airplane, the bicycle, the train, or the boat? Go to the library, or check the World Wide Web for more details about your favorite.

BOOKS

Alexander Graham Bell. Famous Lives (series). Davidson (Gareth Stevens)

Ask Isaac Asimov (series). How Do Airplanes Fly? How Do Big Ships Float? How Does a TV Work? Asimov (Gareth Stevens)

Be An Inventor. Taylor (Harcourt, Brace, Jovanovich)

Bicycle Racing. Nielsen (Carniva

Cameras and Photography. Hawsby and Chisholm (Educational Development Corporation)

Click! A Story about George Eastman. Mitchell (Carolrhoda)

Electricity. Toy Box Science (series). Ollerenshaw and Triggs (Gareth Stevens)

Iron Horse —Iron Man. Dreher (Railhead)

Isaac Asimov's New Library of the Universe (series). Asimov (Gareth Stevens)

Man Flies On. Althea (Cambridge University Press)

Measure Up with Science (series). Distance, Speed, Time, Size. Walpole (Gareth Stevens)

Our Century (series). (Gareth Stevens)

The Satellite Atlas. Flint (Gareth Stevens)

Simple Science Projects. Williams (Gareth Stevens)

The Space Telescope. Lampton (Watts)

TV and Video. Irvine (Watts)

VIDEOS

History of Flight: Balloons. (National Audiovisual Center)

Industrial Revolution. (Educational Video Network)

Isaac Asimov's New Library of the Universe Videos. Piloted Space Flights. The Earth's Moon. (Gareth Stevens)

Television: Line by Line. (International Film Bureau)

Trains. (Film Ideas)

WEB SITES

www.it.rit.edu/~gehouse/index.html

www.ideas.wis.net/cyif1.html

www.gleim.com/Aviation/IntroAirplanes.html

quest.arc.nasa.gov/interactive/hst.html/

PLACES TO VISIT

George Eastman House
International Museum of Photography and Film
900 East Avenue
Rochester, NY 14607

Inventure Place
National Inventors Hall of Fame
221 South Broadway Street
Akron, OH 44308-1505

EAA Air Adventure Museum
3000 Poberezny Road
Oshkosh, WI 54903-3065

Ontario Science Centre
770 Don Mills Road
Don Mills, Ontario M3C 1T3

Museum of Transportation
3015 Barrett Station Road
St. Louis, MO 63122

Astrocentre
Royal Ontario Museum
100 Queen's Park
Toronto, Ontario M5S 2C6

INDEX